ENGAGE THE BRAIN

ENGAGE
THE
BRAIN

ASCD MEMBER BOOK

Many ASCD members received this book as a
member benefit upon its initial release.

Learn more at: **www.ascd.org/memberbooks**

ENGAGE THE BRAIN

How to Design for Learning That Taps into the Power of Emotion

ASCD

Alexandria, VA USA

ALLISON POSEY

1703 N. Beauregard St. • Alexandria, VA 22311-1714 USA
Phone: 800-933-2723 or 703-578-9600 • Fax: 703-575-5400
Website: www.ascd.org • E-mail: member@ascd.org
Author guidelines: www.ascd.org/write

Deborah S. Delisle, *Executive Director*; Stefani Roth, *Publisher*; Genny Ostertag, *Director, Content Acquisitions*; Allison Scott, *Acquisitions Editor*; Julie Houtz, *Director, Book Editing & Production*; Jamie Greene, *Associate Editor*; Judi Connelly, *Associate Art Director*; Masie Chong, *Senior Graphic Designer*; Kelly Marshall, *Senior Production Specialist*; Mike Kalyan, *Director, Production Services*; Circle Graphics, *Typesetter*; Trinay Blake, *E-Publishing Specialist*

All web links in this book are correct as of the publication date below but may have become inactive or otherwise modified since that time. If you notice a deactivated or changed link, please e-mail books@ascd.org with the words "Link Update" in the subject line. In your message, please specify the web link, the book title, and the page number on which the link appears.

PAPERBACK ISBN: 978-1-4166-2628-2   ASCD product #119015
PDF E-BOOK ISBN: 978-1-4166-2630-5; see Books in Print for other formats.

Quantity discounts: 10–49, 10%; 50+, 15%; 1,000+, special discounts (e-mail programteam@ascd.org or call 800-933-2723, ext. 5773, or 703-575-5773). For desk copies, go to www.ascd.org/deskcopy.

ASCD Member Book No. FY19-2 (Nov. 2018 PSI+). ASCD Member Books mail to Premium (P), Select (S), and Institutional Plus (I+) members on this schedule: Jan, PSI+; Feb, P; Apr, PSI+; May, P; Jul, PSI+; Aug, P; Sep, PSI+; Nov, PSI+; Dec, P. For current details on membership, see www.ascd.org/membership.

Library of Congress Cataloging-in-Publication Data

Names: Posey, Allison, author.
Title: Engage the brain : how to design for learning that taps into the power of emotion / Allison Posey.
Description: Alexandria, VA, USA : ASCD, [2019] | Includes bibliographical references and index.
Identifiers: LCCN 2018025715 (print) | LCCN 2018041788 (ebook) | ISBN 9781416626305 (PDF) | ISBN 9781416626282 (pbk.)
Subjects: LCSH: Learning, Psychology of. | Cognitive styles in children. | Emotions and cognition. | Affective education.
Classification: LCC LB1060 (ebook) | LCC LB1060 .P66 2019 (print) | DDC 370.15/23—dc23
LC record available at https://lccn.loc.gov/2018025715

26 25 24 23 22 21 20 19   1 2 3 4 5 6 7 8 9 10 11 12

Education is the kindling of a flame, not the filling of a vessel.

—Socrates

Acknowledgments

In graduate school, my professor David Rose commented that "at its core, teaching is emotional work." I was overwhelmed with this phrase because it captured exactly what I had experienced as a teacher. I loved my teaching jobs, but every year I burned out. I experienced how engagement mattered for my students and their learning, but I did not know how to design for it outside of trying to have lots of fun activities. Recently, in my work with classroom educators, I find that most want to focus on strategies to support engagement; they see engagement as the biggest barrier to learning. I hope this book empowers educators to design for engagement, because we know that in order to learn, we must first be engaged. I hope it also empowers educators to design for their own emotional teaching journeys.

As I reflect on who to thank, I have to start with David Rose. With his mentorship in graduate school and leadership at CAST, I have learned so much about the role of emotion for learning. He is the first I know to use the phrase "emotional design." Universal Design for Learning gave me a new way to define engagement that aligned to my goals as an educator: recruiting interest, sustaining effort and persistence, and self-regulation. This was powerful. I want to thank my CAST colleagues for deepening my understanding of emotions and design for learning, especially Rachel Currie-Rubin (the other half of my brain), Sami Daley, Gabbie Schlichtmann, San Johnston, Kim Ducharme, and Yvonne Domings, and the CAST cadre who always inspire me, including Loui Lord Nelson, who encouraged me to keep writing.

Thank you to the educators from around the world who I have gotten to collaborate with and brainstorm about learning and design. I hope that we continue to share and build strategies so that we can engage every learner in equitable, inclusive, meaningful, and challenging learning opportunities. Thank you to my graduate school professors, Tina Grotzer, Todd Rose, and Kurt Fischer, as your work helped me work to frame the neuroscience-to-education conversation. I want to thank the educators and students from the schools where I have been privileged to teach, as it was with you that I gained real experiences about the central role of emotion for learning and realized that there is nothing more satisfying than an "a-ha" moment! It happens in unique ways and at different times for each of us.

All along the way, my incredible family and friends listened to my ideas at all hours of the day, shared their own learning experiences, and encouraged and celebrated the journey with me. Griffin and Ella, thank you for every trip to Natick and for inspiring me to keep growing each day. Thank you, Keith, for talking through how our fields overlap at all hours. I am so grateful to have you in my life. Thank you, Ms. Pickerel, my 1st grade teacher, who started me on this journey by showing me that even a walk down the hallway can and should be fun.

INTRODUCTION

It came down to the final few seconds of Super Bowl XLVI. New England Patriots quarterback Tom Brady had one final chance to pass the ball for a touchdown that would make the Patriots the Super Bowl champions for the 2011 season. It had been a close game against the New York Giants. The Patriots led 10–9 at halftime and were still ahead, 17–15, with two minutes left in the game. However, in the last minute, the Giants scored a touchdown, putting them ahead by 4. The Patriots needed a touchdown to win. On this cold Sunday night in February 2012 in Boston, I was glued to the television as Brady sent a final "Hail Mary" pass down the field. It was incomplete. The Patriots lost, and I went upstairs and collapsed into tears.

I am not a football fan. I don't think I have ever actually watched an entire game, but I was devastated by the outcome of this particular game. You see, the headmaster of the school where I was a teacher had said that if the Patriots won, the school would be closed the following day. I would get one day off from teaching my high school science classes—a retreat in the middle of the cold, bleak, break-less part of the school year. My newfound enthusiasm for football was unbelievably passionate! I was confident in the pundits' predictions. The Patriots would win, and I would spend my Monday indulging in a slow breakfast, sipping hot coffee, and reading my favorite book in my pajamas.

As shocked as the Patriots were in defeat, I too fell into a similar state of shock that had nothing to do with football: I had to go to school the next day. Logically I knew that this one school day—seven hours—was not that significant in overall scope. I had already prepared the lesson, and now, with a regular Monday class session, we would not fall behind in content. Why was I so upset? I really liked my job, I had an incredible group of motivated students, and I was passionate about the content I was teaching. Emotions seemed to overrule my logic, and my tears continued to flow.

Looking back, I reflect on my Super Bowl meltdown with a statement from David Rose, a developmental neuropsychologist and long-time faculty member at Harvard University's Graduate School of Education: "Teaching is emotional work." My reaction to the Patriots' loss was not about dissatisfaction with my job, career, or overall direction in life. Instead, the emotion of teaching had overwhelmed me, and I was drained. By February, those seven hours of relief from the emotional energy required for effective teaching had become a magical oasis, a reprieve that I was desperately craving.

I started noticing more examples of the central role of emotion in teaching. At an opening faculty meeting I remember a second-year teacher sharing her concern: "I love the students, but I hope I can make it through this year." That was all she could say before she choked up with tears. Even though I have been in education for almost two decades, I still get those pangs of anxiety, butterflies in my stomach, and apprehension at the start of the school year. I could feel her anticipation of the emotional energy required for effective teaching.

Many people think that they can teach, perhaps because they have been students in school themselves or because they have expertise in a subject they enjoy. Often that confidence is overblown. A very successful Washington, DC, attorney joined a high school faculty to teach civics after a 20-year career in law. He was exhausted by spring break of his first year and was unable to return to the classroom. He commented that his time as a teacher had been the most challenging six months of his life. Content expertise is only a sliver of teaching; the rest is emotional work.

The Purpose of This Book

The purpose of this book is to inform educators about the brain science related to emotion and learning, and, more important, to offer strategies to apply these understandings to their own teaching. Although many of the approaches I describe will be familiar, integrating the lens of emotion and the brain may be a new concept. As an educator, I had been trained in how to deliver content and organize my lessons, but I had not been taught how to design learning experiences that support emotions for learning. I hope this book empowers educators to incorporate emotional design for learning.

Brain science shows that emotion is essential for learning. The title of an article by Immordino-Yang and Damasio (2007)—"We Feel, Therefore We Learn"—captures the essence of the point. In addition, Van Gorp and Adams (2012) describe how "emotion paints our understandings, commands our attention, dominates decision-making, and can enhance our memories" (p. 4). If emotion networks of the brain are damaged, memory, perception, and certain other cognitive processes remain intact; however, learning is compromised. Without the ability to feel emotional responses, individuals are left unable to make even a simple cognitive decision, such as what to wear in the morning. For patients who sustain damage to the ventromedial prefrontal cortex, their "social behavior was compromised, making them oblivious to the consequences of their actions, insensitive to others' emotions, and unable to learn from their mistakes" (Immordino-Yang

& Damasio, 2007, p. 4). Skills essential for academic success also rely on emotion. Indeed, many aspects of cognition, including attention, memory, and social skills, are intertwined within emotions. For rigorous learning, students must be engaged.

Educators play a critical role in designing environments for engaged learning. They have choices for how to design in ways that build background knowledge and so students can show what they know. Educators have a choice about how to make the material relevant, relatable, and engaging. However, many still believe that emotions are superfluous for learning and actually interfere with the learning process. I have heard educators say, "Check your emotions at the door," "I do not teach for emotion; I teach content," or "I want my lessons to be rigorous, so I don't have time to worry about whether it also engages them." Additionally, I have heard students say, "School is not for enjoyment; it is for learning." These comments are misguided. Now that we can peer inside the brain, we see that emotion networks are interconnected with cognitive networks—not separate systems. Emotions enable us to learn.

This book offers practical strategies for educators of all levels and content areas to design learning experiences that incorporate emotion for learning. Student brains are not simply waiting to be filled with information. Instead, students' emotions must be activated, attention captured, and memory supported, so that learning becomes something that is intrinsically motivated and can be transferred to real-world experiences.

How This Book Is Organized

This book presents six approaches, or strategies, for designing learning environments that tap into the power of emotion:

- Activate physiology with clear goals and purposeful, aligned options. Make it relevant.

- Design for variability using Universal Design for Learning (UDL).

- Foster the development of brain networks in the brain by modeling, reflecting, and providing feedback.

- Captivate attention with routines, novelty, and autonomy.

- Scaffold memory networks with multisensory and emotional connections. Work to reduce cognitive load.

- Intrinsically motivate using theories of flow and self-determination. Communicate about emotions.

Each of the book's first six chapters covers one of the strategies in depth. Chapter 1 explores how emotions activate the body's physiology for learning and acknowledges how the range of student activation can become overwhelming for an educator to address with dozens of learners in their classes each day. Chapter 2 discusses variability and how the Universal Design for Learning framework can be leveraged to reduce barriers and support the predictable range of learners. The brain's remarkable ability to change due to interactions with the environment is explored in Chapter 3. Chapters 4 and 5 go beyond basic physiological activation to examine how emotions direct and captivate attention and support memory. Ultimately, the goal is for learners to be intrinsically motivated, and Chapter 6 offers strategies to design for this deep level of engagement. Chapter 7 focuses on the teacher perspective and considers how to design professional environments that will sustain educators' own emotional energy for teaching.

This book challenges educators to go beyond being a subject-area or grade-level expert who knows how to deliver information and to think of themselves as designers who craft experiences that first value and address emotion for learning. It also recognizes that teaching itself is emotional work.

How can educators design for engagement? How can we leverage brain research to inform our design? Instead of educators saying, "My students are not engaged," this book challenges them to ask, "How does the design of the learning environment engage my students?" The strategies described can be applied to any content, grade level, or context, including after-school programs, outdoor learning, coaching, online courses, higher education courses, or home schooling. Share ideas from this book or use the Reflect and Discuss questions within each chapter for professional learning group (PLG) or department team discussions.

Defining Terms: *Emotion* and *Engagement*

Two key terms used in this book are *emotion* and *engagement*. The definition of *emotion* used in this book is largely informed by the work of Lisa Feldman Barrett (2017a) and aligns with growing evidence that there are not isolated emotion centers in the brain that are waiting to be activated. Instead, emotions are a result of changes that take place in the brain and body physiology due to an interaction with the environment and that are related to previous experiences. For example, you may describe the emotion "happy" when you eat a sweet chocolate dessert. The first bite activates changes in your brain and body, such as taste receptors that trigger dopamine release, giving you that "I liked that; let's do that again" feeling. You may have memories of eating chocolate as a child that contribute to what you have learned and to how you are appraising this current situation. The context and background experiences really matter for how we interpret the changes of our brain and body and for how we ultimately interpret and label the emotion. Therefore, when I say, "I am happy," you and I may have a shared understanding of what this means based on our own experiences. Emotions are constructed and learned, and together we build a shared language for understanding what these emotions are and mean.

Engagement involves increased focus, participation, and interest. We may turn our head to pay attention, close our eyes to concentrate, or lean in to be more present in the moment. We may be more willing to sustain effort and persist through challenges when we are engaged. I hope you engage with the content in this book in both active and reflective ways. You may draw pictures, take notes, have discussions, and try some ideas in your classrooms!

Use the following example to reflect on the distinction between emotion and engagement. Imagine you witness a car accident—a minor fender-bender that happens right in front of you. You may respond emotionally to the accident as your heart and breath rate increase and your palms become sweaty. You interpret the emotion or feeling to be a mix of dread (Is everyone all right?) and frustration (I might be late now) based on past experiences with this kind of situation. You engage in the event with alertness and direct attention to the scene, preparing to help out or reroute your drive. Others who witness the accident may have different physiological changes triggered by their previous experiences. They may engage in the situation differently and use different words to describe their emotions.

The Connection to Brain Science

This book supports the growing interest in and emphasis on "brain-based" teaching strategies and a need for attending to the social-emotional needs of learners. Although it can be argued that research from a controlled neuroscience laboratory is too rigid to be applied to the dynamic, bustling environment of a classroom, connections between the two fields are important to bridge. To educate effectively, we must understand the learning brain. We can strengthen the neuroscience-to-education loop, as educators are in the business of building brains, and we can inform neuroscientists of important observations or problems of practice for further study. A community college instructor once told me, "If you teach about the brain, it will help [teachers] better understand why certain practices work more than others."

Four overarching themes about the brain recur throughout the book:

- Emotions are central for learning.
- There is a tremendous range or variability in how individuals learn. There is even variability in learning preferences within the same individual at different times; no individual has a fixed learning style.
- The brain has incredible plasticity and can change based on interactions with the environment.
- Background and experience really matter for learning.

Reflect and Discuss

Throughout this book you will find text boxes that ask you to reflect on and discuss the main points that have been covered. You can begin that process by asking yourself or discussing with a professional learning group the following questions:

1. Reflect on something you learned well in school. How did emotion play a role in that learning?
2. What emotion design strategies do you already incorporate into your learning environment to engage students?
3. Review the four overarching themes about the brain listed at the end of this Introduction. Which resonate? Which are new to you or different from what you may have believed?
4. How would you describe your emotions right now? How are you engaging in the reading experience? How is the design of your environment supporting (or not supporting) your engagement?

1

ACTIVATE LEARNING

Emotions are not just messy toddlers in a china shop, running around breaking and obscuring delicate cognitive glassware. Instead, they are more like the shelves underlying the glassware; without them cognition has less support.

—Mary Helen Immordino-Yang and Antonio Damasio,
We Feel, Therefore We Learn

Brain Research	Design Strategies
• The brain actively predicts how to budget energy based on previous experiences. • Brain networks related to emotion are widespread and diffuse, activating the body's physiological and cognitive processes. • Learning needs sufficient activation.	• Clarify the intended goal for each part of a lesson. • Ensure learning goals are relevant and meaningful for students. • Design the context in a flexible way, with resources and options for active learning that align with the intended goal.

Educator Dilemma: Drew was in my neuroscience elective, a three-week, intensive class for "gifted and talented" high school students. His motivation to learn the content was insatiable; in fact, we had to make rules for mandatory study breaks so that he would eat, exercise, and socialize. After the first week of class, Drew had read the entire college-level textbook, and it was evident he understood many of the topics from the rich conversations he initiated. He was curious about long-term potentiation and understanding neural changes that occurred during classical conditioning. However, when I collected his first test, it was completely blank. He had not answered a single question. I wondered what had happened. How could he have learned so much information but been unable to share any of it on an assessment? I asked myself, "Why is his test blank? He knows the content, so is this a problem of engagement?" In what ways does this educator dilemma resonate with you?

Emotion: The Activator of Physiology

In every moment of every day, your brain and body are subconsciously working to appraise your current situation. Are you basically OK in this moment? How much energy does your nervous system need to expend to handle the demands of the situation? Consider what is happening in your current surroundings: Is it loud or dark? Is there someone to interact with? Is there food to eat? Do you need to run away? Do you need to learn something? Now reflect on your body's internal state: Are you hot or cold? Do you need to shift your weight to relieve pressure on your back? Is your heart rate sufficient for the oxygen levels in your blood? Are you digesting food? Thankfully you don't need to actively monitor many of these states, but your nervous system does in every moment of every day.

In classic neuroscience, this appraisal of the body has been described as being like a loop. Incoming sensory information from the external environment (and internal body systems) was sent to, processed, and evaluated by the brain, which led to an appropriate motor output response. For example, if there was a buzzing mosquito near your arm, the sensory input was perceived and processed by your brain, which coordinated a response to shoo it away. This process maintains the body in a state of balance, or *homeostasis*.

Current understanding of the brain shows a much more dynamic process in play than this simple loop. It turns out that your brain is a phenomenal prediction machine. Instead of just waiting for incoming sensory information, it is actively appraising each moment to anticipate what you may need. For example, when I go out into the backyard in the summer, my brain is already predicting that the outdoor environment may include a lot of mosquitos, and it is evaluating the energy that will be required to maintain homeostasis within this context. It may begin to release glucose to my muscles, preparing for a lot of swatting. I may perceive the presence of a mosquito and shoo at it, only to find that there is not one there. My brain directs attention to pertinent stimuli from the environment to help achieve my goals, and it ignores unnecessary information, such as the sound of my neighbor's leaf blower or cars driving by. My nervous system predicts and budgets energy appropriately for that situation based on previous experiences and the goals of the situation.

Shifting to a school context, imagine you enter a classroom and are told, "Today we are going to research and deliver an oral report on spiders." How do you appraise this situation? Based on prior experiences, your brain begins to make predictions. It may evaluate this situation positively: "I have a pet spider and I love talking in front of the class." Others may appraise this situation negatively: "I dislike spiders. I hate talking in this class because kids tease me and this teacher does not like me." Your appraisal is based on your past experiences as well as experiences in this particular context. It is aligned to the targeted goal or task at hand. The appraisal occurs at both a conscious and a subconscious level, and you may identify the emotion in different ways, perhaps as being "excited and ready to go" or "slightly agitated and negative." Your brain predicts the energy demands it may require for this task in this context, and this prediction influences what you pay attention to, how you execute the tasks, and ultimately how you engage and learn in that moment.

Reflect and Discuss

Pause for a moment and reflect on a single moment in your learning environment.

- Describe the context (environment). What are your students doing?
- What previous experiences have students had in this context that may influence how their brains are making predictions about the energy they need to expend to achieve the intended learning goal?

Ultimately, at the core of these appraisals are emotions. Emotion networks are widespread throughout the brain and intricately connect to the body's physiological systems as well as to higher-order cognitive networks. Emotion networks connect with survival centers that influence heart rate, breath rate, and blood pressure. If you are nervous about presenting the spider report in front of peers, you may perceive an increase in activity in these systems and describe the situation by noting, "My palms are sweaty and I feel nervous." The physiological arousal that accompanies emotion also activates attention systems and motivates the body to take action. It recruits motor systems that move muscles and direct actions. Brain networks involved in memory formation, goal setting, planning, reasoning, and problem solving are recruited. These lead to observable behaviors. At the center of this abundance of activity is the emotional appraisal.

Each learner in a classroom will appraise and feel each situation differently based on the goals, the context, and the individual's previous experiences. Each will have unique brain activation and physiological responses, even if behaviors appear consistent. For example, some students may start in on the task and seem to be working in a fairly consistent way, even though their appraisals, internal processes, and predictions vary in a multitude of ways: one student may have just had a fight with a friend and may not be paying any attention to the lesson, another may have never done an oral report before and be overwhelmed, and another may be an experienced actor who is completely comfortable in front of an audience and cannot wait to give the report. For an educator, this variability can be a challenge and seem overwhelming to address in the classroom. How can you possibly be aware of all of the different appraisals and subsequent emotions of each learner in each situation? How can we design to address this range?

Designing for Emotion

Every learning event in our classrooms is appraised in this conscious and unconscious "is this good or bad for me" way. The appraisal causes a shift in physiology—perhaps heart rate and blood pressure increase, pupils dilate, and palms sweat. Individuals may consciously recognize these shifts ("I feel nervous"), or the shifts may be subconscious and manifest in an upset stomach. In addition, higher-order brain systems are activated, such as memory and planning centers. ("Remember that last oral presentation when I used index cards and practiced in front of the mirror? That worked great!" or "Last time I stuttered and no one could hear me. What options can help me this time?") As each learner progresses through the day, the brain predicts and appraises every situation as it relates to previous experiences and the current context. In this way, the brain budgets the body's energy resources to drive perception and prepare for action.

The first step in designing learning experiences for this range of emotional appraisal is to clarify the intended learning goal. For example, the focus of this learning experience may primarily be to *deliver* an oral report, with less emphasis on learning facts about spiders or learning to compile information into a report. Those other skills may be of focus in other lessons and may actually be a barrier for some to achieve the oral component. Once the target goal is clarified, focus on it! Identify the subskills required to effectively deliver an oral report and share those expectations with students. What does it mean to deliver a superb oral report? What do "expert" presenters do? Clarify the expectations so students know what they are going for. When you zero in on the goal, the brain knows what to focus on and how to predict and direct energy for attention, planning, and action.

Once you have clarified the goal for the task, reflect on the relevancy of the goal. Why does it matter? What is the purpose? Is there a meaningful connection you can make so that students will care? Because emotions are at the core of the brain's appraisals, connecting the goals to authentic and relevant experiences will help students activate their physiology and appraise the situation positively. It will invite curiosity, so they might take notice or want to explore more.

Finally, it is important to offer a few choices related to the identified goal. Because each learner brings unique experiences and backgrounds to each situation, offering even two options can help the nervous system appraise the situation in a more positive way. For example, if the goal is to deliver an effective oral report and meaningful connections are made to how this skill is relevant, then consider how you can offer a few options for students to select as they work to achieve that goal. For example, there may be the option to deliver the presentation to the class or to make a video of their presentation, like a news report. Another option might be to allow them to select any topic for the oral report. You might offer the option to use a graphic organizer and to preview the rubric that will be used to assess the oral delivery. Whatever the options are, the focus of the materials and methods should align with the intended goal, so learners are supported to get to high-level skills and can more positively appraise the context as one that is encouraging them to engage in the learning.

The Physiology of Emotion

When you feel an emotion—any emotion, such as disgust, excitement, or anger—your body goes through a range of physiological changes associated with the sympathetic nervous system, including changes in heart rate, galvanized sweat response, pupil dilation, blood pressure, digestion, and breath rate. Glucose, or sugar, can be triggered to be released from storage to deliver the energy needed for your muscles to move your body, whether it is to avert the oral report and talk with friends or to practice the presentation. A number of chemicals help prepare the body for action. Adrenaline mobilizes the body, increasing heart rate and blood pressure, and enlarging blood vessels—a combination that gives the skin a "blushing," reddish hue. It helps "tag" events for memory, so years later you might recall this spider presentation. Cortisol, a stress hormone, releases blood sugar that mobilizes muscles and helps with metabolism and immune function. It travels throughout the brain and body and therefore has a broad impact. Note that in prolonged amounts, cortisol is the chemical that can be actually become toxic to the hippocampus, the region of the brain fundamental to learning.

This physiology of emotional activation has remained fundamentally the same over thousands of years of evolution: the system that helped us survive on the savannah is the same system that is active today in our classrooms. However, today, instead of responding to an approaching tiger, students respond to events such as taking tests, reading, public speaking, researching, or choosing where to sit for lunch. The physiology of a student in a classroom can be as intense as it would be if he were escaping a tiger. In fact, physiological measures from a group of elementary school students reading a passage aloud to their peers were found to be as extreme as someone running from a tiger: stress hormones were high, galvanized skin responses peaked, and heart rate soared. The teacher, reflecting on this research, was understandably surprised and said, "I never thought of asking students to read aloud to the class as being like tigers in the room for some students."

Similarly, a teacher's physiology will be activated differently throughout the course of a school day, making predictions tied to previous experiences with different students, job responsibilities, or interactions with parents and colleagues. Both real and imagined stimuli spark changes in physiology, initiating changes that prepare the body to achieve the goals. Worrying about the upcoming spider presentation or parent-teacher conference can have similar effects on the physiology as the actual event. We learn to describe these changes in brain and body physiology in these different contexts as emotions, and we engage in the situations accordingly.

Recap, Reflect, and Discuss

In any moment, our nervous system prepares our body to take action based on the current goal, the context, and previous experiences. The emotions associated with that appraisal affect our engagement, attention, and actions.

With this in mind, consider the following questions for reflection and discussion:

1. In what ways do you clarify goals, make them relevant, and offer a few options to support those goals?
2. What events might be "like tigers" for your learners during your lessons or in your context?

An Activation Model

A little activation of physiology is good for learning—in fact, it is necessary to kick-start the body to attention and action. However, as in the so-called Goldilocks syndrome, too little activation can result in apathy and boredom, whereas too much activation can lead to stress and anxiety. Returning to the example of the oral report on spiders, one student may appraise the task as incredibly boring. That student's heart rate and breath rate might be low, and cognitive networks such as attention and memory would be minimally active. Without enough activation, undesired behaviors may result, such as an incomplete draft of the speech, a dearth of research, or a poor delivery.

By contrast, another student's appraisal of this assignment may result in stress. He might be uncomfortable thinking about spiders and is nervous at the thought of presenting in front of the class. His heart rate and sweat level may increase; cognitive centers may not function as efficiently as they normally would. Too much activation of physiology diminishes cognitive processes such as attention and memory. This state leads to less conceptual flexibility or creativity; emotions overrule cognition. It may also result in undesirable actions, such as standing speechless during the presentation, or having shaking muscles and a cracking voice, or delivering the speech poorly. Notice that sometimes the observed behavior—in this case, poor delivery— may be similar for the two students, even though their emotional appraisals differ. Most students will fall on a continuum somewhere between these extremes, and the challenge for educators is that each student's activation system will be different in response to events in the classroom.

A "one-size-fits-all" lesson is unlikely to address the range of emotional appraisal and subsequent physiological activation of the students in the class. When we have students do the same task in the same way and at the same time, we are not designing for the range of students we know we have. To overcome this challenge, educators should follow the suggestions mentioned earlier: offer a clear goal, a relevant connection that addresses the question "why does this matter," and a few options within the lesson to support the intended lesson goal. These elements guide the nervous system toward the appropriate sensory and motor actions and support engagement for the learning task. As shown in Figure 1.1, which illustrates the "activation model," finding the right point on the spectrum between low emotional activation (boredom) and high emotional activation (anxiety) by offering relevant options for attaining the goal is the key to student cognition. Having an option to work with a peer, to use a graphic organizer, to see a model example, or to get to choose the animal to research can shift appraisal of the task. However, it is essential to have the learning target (goal, objective) clarified so that you are able to optimize the flexible options that you offer. Rubrics and assessments should focus on and highlight the necessary skills to achieve the goals, and even though learners begin in different places, each can progress toward the same goal. One educator's experience illustrates the potential benefits: "My learning goal was for students to write a comparative essay. I decided to let students choose their topics, instead of using my topics. One student who had not written much all year actually wrote two pages comparing pancakes and waffles."

FIGURE 1.1 | **Activation Model**

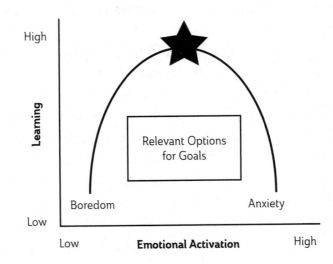

Here is an example of how a 5th grade teacher incorporated a clear goal into her lesson so she could integrate targeted, flexible options to support the range of student activation during the learning event. As she had done before, Ms. McNabb had the local science museum bring a stargazing bubble to her classroom. Having the bubble in the classroom was usually a memorable event, but she started to think about the range of activation of her students and how to incorporate clear goals and purposeful options into the experience to enhance the learning. Many students became very excited when they saw the bubble and eagerly entered, but some were more reluctant to go into the dark, enclosed space with their energized classmates.

First, Ms. McNabb clarified the learning goal and discussed with the students why it mattered: "Have any of you ever told stories about the patterns you see in the stars at night? Today we will find a few different constellations so you can tell what season it is and even find your own zodiac constellation by looking at the stars." Then she realized that not all students necessarily had to enter the bubble; some could choose to watch the lesson through a window in the bubble or quietly use headphones and a video to learn the constellations. She recorded the stargazing session and posted it to her website so students could watch the video on their own, which helped students who were absent during the class period as well as those who missed some of the information during the session. She also invited students to create their own stories about the constellations instead of just learning the ancient tales. She noted that these goal-driven options in the lesson led to deeper levels of observation, discussion, and learning. More students seemed engaged.

These small modifications in lesson design optimized options and relevancy in support of the target goal. Some of these options were already present in the lesson, but the activation model helped Ms. McNabb reflect on why some of her teaching strategies worked (or did not work). She thought more about how the purposeful options for the clear, relevant goal helped students be in an active, focused state for learning. Not all students needed to do the same thing at the same time.

Understanding how the brain is an active predictor helps us understand why we need to set clear, meaningful goals. Thinking about the activation model helps us reflect on why we need to provide a few purposeful options to support the range of learners in our teaching contexts.

Invite learners to use the activation model themselves to reflect and share their thoughts about their learning choices. How do they initially appraise a learning goal? How do options for relevancy and learning choices change their appraisal and engage them more meaningfully in the task? Learners can become more metacognitive about options that work best or that do not work well for them as they pursue the goal.

In summary, based on previous experiences, a learner's brain appraises the energy and resources it may need to expend in a given context. Emotion networks are central to both physiology and cognitive centers; emotion is at the core of learning. Having a clear goal that matters and relevant options in the environment can shift emotional appraisal into a more active, directed state for learning.

Recap, Reflect, and Discuss

We need some activation to initiate learning, but each individual appraises a situation in a different way, based on previous experiences and the current context. Educators can design for this range by clarifying the goal, making it relevant, and integrating options that support the range of emotional activation.

With this in mind, consider the following questions for reflection and discussion:

1. What previous experiences might students have in your subject area or class that affect how they are predicting and appraising your context?
2. How can you work to clarify goals and to make them relevant?
3. How can you use the activation model and plan a few flexible options for the range of learners?

How Emotions Tie the Knot for Learning

An adult sticks her tongue out at a baby, and the baby mimics the action by sticking out her tongue as well. The adult coos with praise. This interaction between the child and the adult included an emotional response, and we know that learning took place because the next time the baby saw the same adult, she stuck out her tongue again. Learning happened through the interaction of the baby with the adult, and even in such a simple example, it is clear that emotion played a key role.

Learning includes the process of gaining information from the environment or body systems (the child sees the adult stick out her tongue), actively trying out and incorporating the skills or behaviors (the child tries to stick out her tongue), and then applying them in novel circumstances (the child sticks out her tongue again, even without the adult initiating). The child in this example was actively engaged in the new experience, not just passively receiving information. The next time the child was in a similar context, the brain had anticipated and appraised the situation, which led to purposeful actions and behaviors.

For learning to occur, there must be an active interaction between the learner and the learning environment, including the work spaces in the room, the materials and methods of a lesson (e.g., books, technologies, handouts, rubrics, and assessments), and their peers and teachers. The learning environment can include scaffolds or tools and resources that students can use when first learning something but are intended to be gradually released once the learner becomes more proficient at the skill. Like the scaffolding on a building, learning scaffolds are meant to be removed over time. For example, a graphic organizer is a scaffold for writing that may help an individual achieve the writing goal. Over time, the graphic organizer is needed less, but initially it may be important to an individual's appraisal of the writing task. We can apply what we have learned about emotions and learning to this simple scenario, and you can extend it to think about your own classroom. How does designing a simple change in the learning environment—that connects to the intended learning goal, such as a graphic organizer for writing—influence a student's interaction with the environment and appraisal of the situation? How might this encourage more engagement and even risk-taking in the learning?

We learn emotions in much the same way that we learn words and concepts. Take, for example, how we learn the meaning of a dog. We perceive key features of a dog: two ears, four legs, and fur, and it barks. We interact with and share this understanding using language, pictures, and real examples to describe and highlight different kinds of dogs. We learn that a dog can be distinguished from a wolf or cat, which also have two ears, four legs, and fur. We learn best about dogs when we are able to have a contextualized, active experience with them (i.e., petting, smelling, and playing with them). Similarly, when we learn about our emotions, we begin to recognize the changes that take place in our brain and body due to interactions with the environment. We connect these changes to previous experiences we may have had, and we share a deeper meaning and understanding of emotions when we use a common language and share examples and experiences. For example, consider phrases such as "When I read this, I felt sad and there was a lump in my throat," "I was proud of the way she stood up to the bully, and I wanted to cheer," or "The last time I saw that, I laughed and felt happy." Notice how the words for the emotions connect to changes in physiology and are contextualized.

In the classroom, we may hear, "I was nervous when I presented in front of the class. My heart was racing, and I didn't want to talk." When we begin to clarify language for emotion in a learning situation and connect it with a goal, we can then start to design options to support the activation in the context. "Having a friend present with me helped me feel calmer" or "Practicing first with a video camera helped my voice be less shaky." The more we co-construct a language to describe emotions in connection to our body activation in a learning environment, the more effectively we can incorporate "emotional design" for learning.

Chapter Summary

Emotions are essential for learning. The brain's emotion networks connect with basic body survival systems such as heart rate and blood pressure, and they also connect with higher-order cognitive systems such as memory and attention. Perception, action, and behaviors always involve emotion networks. In any situation, the nervous system makes predictions about the energy demands it will have to support and appraises the situation by asking, "Is this good or bad for me?" This appraisal directs perception and action both consciously and subconsciously.

Each learner's system activates in a unique way—too little activation can lead to boredom or apathy, and too much activation can lead to stress or anxiety. The challenge for educators is to support the wide range of activation in a context with a range of learners. To do this, first identify a clear learning target and make it relevant and meaningful for your learners. Then proactively integrate or scaffold a few options into the environment that support learners' progress and achievement of that goal.

Revisiting the Educator Dilemma

Let's return to the anecdote at the start of this chapter, about Drew, a student who demonstrated a high level of comprehension of complex information but did not do well on a written assessment of this material. Using what was discussed in this chapter about the brain's predictive appraisals based on previous experience and the central role of emotion for cognition, there are several ways to reflect on this educator dilemma.

Here is how this teacher thought about some of the strategies from this chapter; how can you make connections from this chapter to your teaching?

- **Know your learners will have a range of background experiences that influence their appraisal of a situation and engagement in the task.** Drew's previous test-taking experiences influenced how his nervous system made predictions and appraised this situation. The testing environment might be "like a tiger" for his physiology, and his body system may be too activated. This can limit memory and cognitive flexibility so he is not able to demonstrate his full understanding in this context.

- **Clarify the goal.** In this case, was the goal to take a written test or to demonstrate knowledge? Depending on the goal, the options available will vary. If the goal were to demonstrate understanding, then it could be through any means. However, the teacher in this example determined the goal to be an understanding of the concepts through writing (a skill that scientists "in the real world" need).

- **Integrate purposeful options in the learning environment to support the goal.** For example, there could be

  ◊ A practice opportunity, which could be completed and reflected upon collaboratively and with formative feedback before the assessment.

  ◊ Flexible seating or time allotted.

  ◊ Headphones made available as an option to reduce distractions from the environment.

  ◊ An opportunity to use notes, textbooks, and other resources. (After all, when scientists communicate information in writing, they are able to use their resources.)

- **Make the learning task relevant.** Clarify why the task is important. For this example, discuss why it is important to be able to communicate what you know with others in a written form. Have students brainstorm when they may be in this kind of situation in the world outside school.

Note that the options should be available for all learners, not just Drew. Such availability allows all learners to build a repertoire of strategies to become experts about their strengths, challenges, and weaknesses. Ultimately, the educator will determine which options are offered and works with students to select strategies that help achieve the goals. This educator dilemma may be used as a model for thinking about learning and the brain through the lens of emotion.

Teacher Connection: 7th Grade Language Arts

Katie Novak, a 7th grade language arts teacher, thinks of building her lessons as being comparable to building a closet of shoes. She knows there will be a range of student emotions and that at any point students can demonstrate different strengths and challenges. For every lesson, activity, or discussion, she clarifies the goal and makes it authentic. She then shares options and strategies (the "closet of shoes") that are available for all students to use as they work toward the goal. She designs options into the classroom for *all* students to use ("a closet of shoes available for everyone").

Dr. Novak shares with her students how different shoes are more appropriate depending on the goal. If the goal is to go hiking in the snow, winter boots are a good choice. However, there can be choice within the category of "boots." Some will prefer boots with fuzzy, warm insides, while others might choose boots with a tough water-proof surface. Either boot will help students reach the goal of hiking outside in winter. When the goal changes—for example, if the goal is now to go out for a fancy dinner—different shoes become more relevant, and students are empowered to make choices that help them reach the goal. One of her students remarked, "Don't you like different shoes? Well, kids like different ways of learning. It is the same thing." Dr. Novak fills her classroom and lesson "closets of shoes" with options and lets students choose what works best for them for that particular activity.

* * * * * * * *

Social Media Connections

@ASCD
@AspenSEAD
#SEL
@KatieNovakUDL

2

DESIGN FOR VARIABILITY

Everybody is a genius. But if you judge a fish by its ability to climb a tree, it will live its whole life believing that it is stupid.

—Albert Einstein

Brain Research	Design Strategies
• Individual nervous systems vary, including nonobvious ways, such as central-peripheral visual fields. • Variability can be an advantage or a disadvantage, depending on the context. • Variability in learning can be predictable in terms of affective, recognition, and strategic networks.	• Provide options for all learners for representation (how information is presented), action and expression (how they can show what they know), and engagement (how they are invested), using the Universal Design for Learning (UDL) guidelines.

Educator Dilemma: Shakira was struggling to decode and comprehend for some of the reading assignments, so her 3rd grade teacher moved her to the Level 2 reading group. The teacher described how Shakira put her head down and looked upset about this decision, even though she assured her that the groups were designed to help students to do their best reading. The teacher felt the Level 2 book was the appropriate level for Shakira, but for the first time she described Shakira as disengaged and that she did not complete the reading. She wondered why Shakira stopped doing the readings when this was a much better level for her. How does this educator dilemma resonate with you?

A Wide Spectrum

Among any group of people, there is a wide range of physical features. Zoom in and consider, for example, the range of hair types: shades of blonde, brunette, black, and red; textures that are frizzy, curly, wavy, or straight; lengths from zero (bald) to incredibly long. We are born with a particular hair type, but it changes over time. Some may be born with a full head of light hair that then becomes dark and curly, and finally thins and whitens. Others may be born completely bald and grow thick dreadlocks that last a lifetime. Some choose to wax, shave, and remove hair, whereas others use extensors or toupées to augment. Hair qualities are not fixed but can change from day to day, perhaps becoming frizzy in humidity, lighter in the sun, flatter after a blow dry, or colored with dye.

Each human trait has a range, from a variety of waist sizes, heights, skin pigments, eye colors, nose shapes, foot sizes, shoulder girths, fingerprints, freckle densities, arm lengths, and more. When we see physical differences, we can design options to accommodate the range. For example, for the multitude of waist sizes, options such as belts, suspenders, pregnancy pouches, or elastic banding are designed to accommodate the spectrum. After a large meal, I notice my own waist size expands and I prefer to be wearing an elastic waist.

Despite this tremendous range in our physical features, we also have, for the most part, a strikingly similar anatomy. For example, our faces typically include one nose, two eyes, a forehead, a mouth, and two cheeks. We have wrists composed of bones aligned in two rows that join with the arm bones. Likewise, our brains have similar structures, such as two hemispheres connected by a *corpus callosum*, a *brain stem* that leads to the spinal column, a *cerebellum* located off the base of the brain, and a folded *cerebral cortex* made up of gray matter and underlying white matter. There is similar regional specialization for perception of visual, auditory, tactile, gustatory, and olfactory stimuli. There are areas devoted to movement, *somatosensory* functions (related to touch sensations such as pressure, pain, and warmth), memory, and executive function. There are areas such as the amygdala involved in experiences of emotions.

These areas do not sit stagnant in isolation but are networked and interconnected in distinct ways that change depending on use. For example, there is an area of the brain called the *fusiform gyrus* that is typically involved in facial recognition. However, the size and inter-connectivity of the fusiform gyrus will vary among individuals. On one extreme, individuals who have congenital or sustained damage to this region have trouble perceiving facial features (a condition called *prosopagnosia*) and might not even be able to recognize their own face. On the other extreme, "super-recognizers" seem to never forget a face. Most people lie somewhere within this range. Depending on how much we work on recognizing and distinguishing faces, this area may become more or less connected.

Differences in our brains are trickier to detect than external physical features because the brain is housed deep within the skull and we cannot see the variance at a glance. Imagine if we could see the variability of our brains; we could design for this like we design for different foot sizes! Too often, however, we expect our students' brains to be mostly the same, but they are not. We expect there will be a "typical" reading level or skill ability, but there is not. We expect there to be a set of distinct learning styles, but there is not. There is unbelievable variability in the interconnectivity and activity of the brain. Each of the brain's roughly 100 billion neurons can form up to 10,000 connections with other neurons; we have the potential for building upwards of one hundred trillion neural connections. Comprehending this massive number is like trying to quantify how many grains of sand there are on Earth; it is more than the number of stars in our galaxy. Our brains are incredibly complex and unique.

The key point that is important for educators is that there is not just one kind of brain or subset of learning styles but variability in our nervous systems in how we perceive, respond to, and engage with our environment. As we saw in Chapter 1, there is variability in how we appraise situations based on our previous experiences and the context. This influences the activation of our body physiology and of our brain networks for learning. In the next section, we will explore a specific example from the visual system that highlights how variability can influence perception in subtle ways that affect learning. Understanding variability enables us to understand why it is essential to design flexible learning environments if we want to support all learners in our classrooms.

Central-Peripheral Vision: An Example of Variability

Take a moment to observe where you are right now. Notice how objects in your direct line of vision are in clear focus, such as the words on this page or your outstretched fist. These are in your central visual field. Then observe how items in your peripheral visual field are blurrier, such as the objects elsewhere in the room or on the wall. You generally know what these objects are, but not their exact detail because they are in the periphery. It turns out, there is variability in the ratio of the central and peripheral visual fields that relates to structural differences in the retina of the eye and that can have a subtle impact on reading.

The retina is a paper-thin sheet on the back of the eye made up of hundreds of thousands of cells called *rods*, which detect light/dark contrast, and *cones*, which detect colors. The combination of input from the rods and cones provides visual information about our surroundings that gets transmitted in different pathways from the optic nerve to subsequent brain regions. The variability in the number of rods and cones and the size of the central visual field has subtle impacts on perception. Consider an example from baseball and astrophysics.

Imagine you are a baseball batter trying to hit a curveball. From your perspective, you start looking at the ball in the pitcher's hand and you want to follow the trajectory of the ball until it hits the bat. However, a curveball arcs so it moves out of the central visual field and into the blurry, peripheral field. If you shift your gaze to try to refocus on the ball, you end up losing focus again because the ball arcs back into the blurry peripheral field. This shift from the central to the peripheral field of view is so fast that it can be difficult to adjust focus and hit the ball accurately. However, if you had a slightly larger central field of view, you would likely keep better focus on the ball and might improve your hitting accuracy. The subtle difference in the central-peripheral visual field can influence perception and skills. (Note that there are many other factors that influence the ability to hit a curveball. This is just an interesting thought exercise about how a subtle variance in our physiology can affect perception and observed behaviors. I am not suggesting that we begin testing for the size of central-peripheral visual fields in baseball players!)

Variability in central-peripheral visual fields can also affect classroom skills, such as reading, in subtle ways. A subset of individuals with dyslexia has, on average, relatively smaller central visual fields. In some contexts, this can be a disadvantage, such as reading text from a book. This skill relies heavily on the central visual field. In other contexts, however, having a slightly smaller central visual field can be advantageous. It turns out that detecting symmetry patterns in radio waves helps identify potential black holes. This kind of reading skill is valued in astrophysics and can be easier with a slightly larger peripheral visual field. Deficits in one context (reading text) can be advantageous in another (reading wave patterns). Note that this example is not suggesting that having dyslexia is an indicator of ability to detect black holes. In addition, connections with dyslexia and reading are multidimensional and beyond the scope of just variability in the central visual field. However, we use this example to highlight how variability can be an advantage or a disadvantage, depending on the context. Context really matters!

A student may demonstrate tremendous reading ability with a partner or when reading about a favorite subject but may not seem as skilled reading aloud or when vocabulary is a barrier. I have seen a student barely mumble through a verbal presentation in a classroom but then deliver a brilliant soliloquy on a theater stage. How might a learning experience be redesigned so that it is appraised more positively for learning?

We need to offer flexible ways to reduce unintended barriers for learning goals in order to support the variability of our learners. For example, if a reading task at hand is about comprehension, then we can offer flexibility for how the text is decoded, such as through the use of an audio version or partner reading. We can look for ways to make the task more relevant and authentic, such as offering a couple of different topics to read. We can observe how these simple design changes can support many different students, including one student who may be tired from a lot of reading in a previous class to another student who may be a strong decoder. When we design flexible, goal-directed environments, we support the variability of the learners in our classrooms and we design for deeper levels of engagement in the task.

Using the UDL Framework to Design for Variability in Three Brain Networks

Brains are as unique as our fingerprints, and with dozens of students to teach and hundreds of lessons to deliver each year, how can educators effectively design contexts that support this full range of variability? Traditionally, we have labeled students according to abilities or disabilities, learning styles, or preferences. The problem is that this simplicity does not recognize the neurological variability that we know exists and does not address the importance of the context for a preference.

Universal Design for Learning (UDL) is a framework that describes predictable variability across three broad brain networks involved in learning: affective, recognition, and strategic. In reality, all three learning networks are heavily interconnected and are all active during learning. However, this model for thinking about the brain, though simplified and limited in some ways, can be a helpful way to anticipate variability in learning and design accordingly. UDL integrates research from neuroscience with researched best practices from the classroom and seeks to reduce unintended barriers from the environment so more learners engage with and achieve the learning goals.

Three UDL principles align to the three brain networks for learning (see Figure 2.1). The Engagement Principle provides guidelines for how to design for variability in affective networks by offering options that recruit interest, sustain effort and persistence, and support self-regulation. The Representation Principle offers suggestions for how to design for variability in recognition networks by incorporating options for perception, language, and comprehension. The Action and Expression Principle informs design for variability in strategic networks by providing options for physical action, expression and communication, and executive function. The intent is not that every UDL guideline be integrated into every lesson but that the goals drive the selective use of the UDL guidelines. The goal is that the widest range of learners be able to access and progress toward the intended learning goal from the start. Because the goals, materials, methods, and assessments vary for each learning experience, UDL looks different in each context, but the mindset behind the design is consistent.

The next sections delve further into each of the UDL guidelines to explore how they can inform design decisions to reduce barriers in the environment to support learner variability. Learners themselves should be involved in the discussion and design so they become more reflective of their own learning processes. Share the three UDL brain networks with students to help them build a language about learning and the brain so they can become more reflective about what they need in order to do their best learning. I find that students feel empowered by the language of UDL. Too often, we tell students of deficits they have, but with UDL, they see that they have all three brain networks necessary for learning. I remember one student remarking, "You mean I have all of these networks in my brain?" With the UDL framework, learners can communicate more effectively about barriers that prevent them from achieving the goal and about resources that best support their learning. They can start to take more charge of their learning.

Design for Variability in Representation Networks

Did you see the viral, internet sensation dress as being black and blue or white and gold? Did you hear *yanny* or *laurel*? Such examples highlight the subtle variability in our representation networks.

FIGURE 2.1 | The Universal Design for Learning (UDL) Guidelines

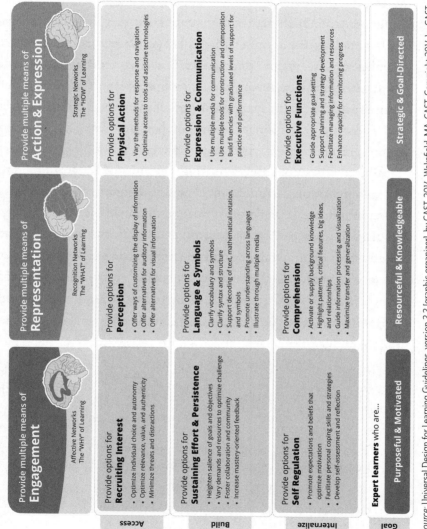

Provide multiple means of
Engagement

Affective Networks
The "WHY" of Learning

Provide options for
Recruiting Interest
- Optimize individual choice and autonomy
- Optimize relevance, value, and authenticity
- Minimize threats and distractions

Provide options for
Sustaining Effort & Persistence
- Heighten salience of goals and objectives
- Vary demands and resources to optimize challenge
- Foster collaboration and community
- Increase mastery-oriented feedback

Provide options for
Self Regulation
- Promote expectations and beliefs that optimize motivation
- Facilitate personal coping skills and strategies
- Develop self-assessment and reflection

Expert learners who are...

Purposeful & Motivated

Provide multiple means of
Representation

Recognition Networks
The "WHAT" of Learning

Provide options for
Perception
- Offer ways of customizing the display of information
- Offer alternatives for auditory information
- Offer alternatives for visual information

Provide options for
Language & Symbols
- Clarify vocabulary and symbols
- Clarify syntax and structure
- Support decoding of text, mathematical notation, and symbols
- Promote understanding across languages
- Illustrate through multiple media

Provide options for
Comprehension
- Activate or supply background knowledge
- Highlight patterns, critical features, big ideas, and relationships
- Guide information processing and visualization
- Maximize transfer and generalization

Resourceful & Knowledgeable

Provide multiple means of
Action & Expression

Strategic Networks
The "HOW" of Learning

Provide options for
Physical Action
- Vary the methods for response and navigation
- Optimize access to tools and assistive technologies

Provide options for
Expression & Communication
- Use multiple media for communication
- Use multiple tools for construction and composition
- Build fluencies with graduated levels of support for practice and performance

Provide options for
Executive Functions
- Guide appropriate goal-setting
- Support planning and strategy development
- Facilitate managing information and resources
- Enhance capacity for monitoring progress

Strategic & Goal-Directed

Access

Build

Internalize

Goal

Representation networks are generally located at the back of the brain and are involved in how we take in information from the environment. There is variability in how we each perceive information from the environment, whether it is what we see, hear, touch, smell, or taste. Differences in visual perception, for example, can be influenced by the number of red-green photoreceptors, how light focuses on the retina, damage to the retina, differences in background experience or language, or sitting too far away from the whiteboard. Variability in audio perception can be influenced by the anatomy of the inner ear or connectivity in the auditory cortex of the brain, by sitting next to a noisy radiator in class, or by having less language exposure. Proactive, intentional design for variability in perception, language, and comprehension creates a learning environment that addresses variability in how our students gain information necessary for learning. It helps our learning environments be more inclusive for all learners, and as one educator noted, "If you are not being intentionally inclusive, you are being exclusive." The UDL Representation Guidelines can be used to address variability in recognition networks by designing with options for the following:

- **Perception.** Options can include both saying and writing key information, providing captioned videos, or offering digital versions of handouts that can then be read aloud, reformatted, or translated.

- **Language, mathematical expressions, and symbols.** Options can include providing graffiti word walls with real-world examples, displaying images, having alt-text for images and other graphics, or using videos.

- **Comprehension.** Options can include using bulleted summaries, concept maps, or highlighted, annotated articles.

Recap, Reflect, and Discuss

Variability occurs throughout the nervous system, including subtle differences such as the number of rods and cones in the eyes and the size of the central and peripheral visual fields. This variability can seem overwhelming for educators to address. Universal Design for Learning is a framework that outlines predictable variability in learning across affective, recognition, and strategic networks of the brain; it can be used to proactively design contexts with options for engagement, representation, and action & expression for targeted goals.

With this in mind, consider the following questions for reflection and discussion:

1. How important is the environment (context) for demonstrating a skill? For example, when was a time that you seemed very skilled in one setting but unskilled at the same task in a different setting? For example, my son describes how effortless it is to shoot a hockey goal during practice, compared to a game.

2. What are ways you think about variability in your learners? How can you design options that anticipate variability before meeting your students to help set a "learning buffet" for the predictable range of learners? For example, the label "English language learner" can be reframed to "variability in language," or the label "ADHD" to "variability in attention."

Design for Variability in Strategic Networks

Paul Smith had cerebral palsy, yet he wanted to be an artist. The physical coordination needed to hold a paintbrush was a barrier for him, so he used another means to paint: a typewriter. He became a masterful artist (Cerebralpalsy.org, n.d.).

Often in education, we require the means to be embedded in tasks. Students must write the essay, build the model, or paint with the brush, for example. However, we all vary in how we best demonstrate knowledge and understanding in different contexts. When we require students to show what they know in just one way, we often create unintended barriers to really understanding what they know. One teacher marveled at the different responses she observed in her students when she offered the option to write or record an understanding of magnetism: "This student hardly wrote a thing, so I did not think he knew much of what we covered. But with the recording, he talked for two minutes about magnetic forces of different objects."

Sometimes the means must be required; for instance, a standardized test may require students to write a comparative essay about Renaissance and Baroque art. Recognize that accomplishing this task requires two skills: (1) knowing how to write a comparative essay, and (2) having knowledge about Renaissance and Baroque art. First, focus deeply on the core understanding about Renaissance and Baroque art by watching videos, having discussions, exploring examples, and summarizing key ideas. Then support students to really know how to craft a comparative essay with options to use a graphic organizer, follow a model example, or choose what they want to compare. Additionally, teach the skills needed to take a standardized test, such as managing time constraints and being able to sit and focus for a long period of time. When we break our goals into subcomponent parts, we are able to more purposefully design options to support students' strategic networks. Ultimately, learners will be more strategic in their ability to integrate skills, content, and self-regulation together.

The UDL Action and Expression Guidelines can be used to address variability in strategic networks by offering options for

- **Physical Action.** Provide options for physical access, such as assistive technologies or options to write, draw, record, construct, or make a video.

- **Expression and Communication.** Offer options for communication and expression, such as sentence starters, use of spelling and grammar checkers, graphic organizers, writing templates, or model (and non-model) examples.

- **Executive Functions.** Optimize options for executive function, such as progress monitoring through the use of checklists or rubrics, or breaking long-term goals into short-term goals. Break multistep problems into sub-component parts.

Just like a GPS helps us be more strategic drivers by telling us how much farther we have to go, when to make turns, and what the next turn will be, our lesson design can help learners be clear about their progression along the way.

Design for Variability in Engagement Networks

How would you feel if you were asked to sing a song in front of an audience? Or to annotate a research-based journal article? Or to do an algebra problem in front of the class on the board? We know that each individual will experience a range of emotions in these different circumstances and that context and background experience greatly influence how we appraise each task. If we feel safe and comfortable with an audience, we may enjoy singing in front of them, even if our singing voice is not very good. We may become engrossed in a research-based journal article if we have sufficient background or can annotate it with a colleague. We may want to try a problem in front of the class if the process is scaffolded.

The affective networks are located primarily in the center of the brain and are heavily interconnected with both the strategic and recognition networks of the cortex, as well as with basic physio-logical systems of the body. As noted in Chapter 1, affective net-works assign value and meaning to a situation based on previous experiences. They influence what we pay attention to and perceive, as well as how we strategize and act in skillful, goal-directed ways. They influence the emotions we feel, as we interpret the changes in our brain and body in a given context.

Two specific brain regions are worth a deeper explanation, as they have been heavily studied in relation to emotion: the *cingulate cortex* and the *amygdala*. Think of the cingulate cortex like a paintbrush, "painting" an experience based on memories and emotions. Imagine a student raises his hand and answers a question incorrectly in a class discussion. The cingulate "paints" this experience by assessing the changes in physiology and lining them up with prior memories in this context. If the environment is supportive and safe for making mistakes, the brain contextualizes positive emotions for this interaction, and this will inform future motivation. Perhaps the mistake is ridiculed by a peer or criticized by the teacher—the cingulate "paints" this experience differently and influences future motivation and action.

Like the cingulate, the amygdala is involved in every experience we have. It acts like a "label machine" to tag and enhance memories, especially emotional memories. It is not an isolated brain region but is networked with other brain regions and is influenced by our body physiology and surrounding environments. For example, you may remember an embarrassing time when you raised your hand and gave an incorrect answer in front of the class. This event was "tagged" by your amygdala with an increase of stress-related hormones and stored in memory systems of the brain, such as the hippocampus. The next time you are in a similar context or if you anticipate raising your hand in class, your brain remembers this "tagged" experience and can use it to actively predict and budget energy to focus attention and drive behavior in this new situation.

Activation of emotion networks such as the amygdala and the cingulate cortex can motivate a learner's actions, with both conscious and unconscious awareness. For example, emotion networks connect with the orbitofrontal cortex for conscious understanding of long-term consequences, such as "If I study this, then I will do well on the test" or "If I work hard on this graphic organizer, then I will write a more organized paper." In addition, some emotion networks are involved in more subconscious processing, such as "The teacher looked at me funny, so I won't do that again" or "I could tell by her tone I was in trouble." These appraisals connect emotions and actions. Damage to these emotional-orbitofrontal connections make even simple decisions seem impossible, as there is no longer an emotional rudder to guide the decision (Bechara, Damasio, Tranel, & Damasio, 2005).

The UDL Engagement Guidelines can be used to design learning experiences to support variability in affective networks. UDL suggests the following:

- **Recruit interest.** Provide options that recruit interest, such as including relevant, authentic examples and real-life "hooks" that are connected to the community. Provide options to minimize threats and distractions, such as quiet or flexible work spaces or options to use headphones. Reflect on how you have created a safe space for learners to advocate for their needs or to take new risks. Encourage student voice and choice in their learning.

- **Sustain effort and persistence.** Offer resources to meet the demands of task. This could include the option to collaborate or work independently (if collaboration is not the goal), to make goals personally relevant, and to have frequent process-oriented feedback toward the goal.

- **Self-regulate.** Offer opportunities for self-regulation, such as emphasizing consistent, high expectations that all learners can be successful. Provide time for self-reflection, and value mistakes as part of the learning process.

Variability in Connections

Workout gyms recognize that there will be variability in how each member best achieves his or her physical training goals. They provide a handful of options in the environment for members to choose from to achieve their physical fitness goals. For example, if someone wanted to work on cardiovascular endurance, she could choose to use the treadmills, swim, or take an exercise class. She could also work with a personal trainer to become more independent with exercise training. Someone in a wheelchair or with a broken foot can still participate in cardiovascular training. Imagine if you went to a gym that had only treadmills. Would you choose that gym?

Current brain-imaging techniques reveal the uniqueness of each brain. Scientists are working to map the *connectome,* or all the connections within the brain, and determine how they relate to functions and behaviors. We see how variable our brains are and realize that there is no "one-size-fits-all" brain structure. Therefore, we should not have a "one-size-fits-all" learning environment. UDL fundamentally shifts the way we design instruction to focus more on proactively reducing barriers in the environment, instead of trying to label and "fix" a learner.

In the following example, a high school history teacher, Mr. Amber, made connections about how he proactively designed his lesson for learner variability. The teaching strategies and methods he integrated were not new, but the approach, which incorporated the UDL guidelines and focused on providing goal-driven options in the environment for all students to use, differed from how he previously designed a lesson with accommodations and modifications for specific students. UDL also helped Mr. Amber reflect on and align the teaching strategies to the learning brain networks, so for each event, he asked himself, "What is my target goal? How have I tried to make it relevant and authentic? How are there options for engagement, representation, and action and expression for my goal?" He used the UDL guidelines to engage in discussions with his students about the learning process and empower them to develop their own learning paths.

Here is how he integrated UDL into the design of a lecture on the causes of the Civil War:

- **Clarify the goal.** Mr. Amber determined that for the 40-minute class period, he wanted students to focus on three factors that led to the Civil War: slavery, the *Dred Scott* decision, and states' rights. He wanted students to (1) know what each of the factors was, (2) express understanding of each in their own way, and (3) understand how the factors contributed to the start of the Civil War. (Recall from Chapter 1 how important it is to make the goals relevant. How could Mr. Amber have made this goal more authentic and meaningful to students? What might be a current situation in their community or school that relates?)

- **Plan for variability in affective networks.** Offer options for engagement. Mr. Amber knew that not all students enjoyed this topic. He worked to invite conversation on how this content was relevant to current events from the school or community. He offered opportunities for students to collaborate around a question at different points during the lecture, to try to co-construct meaning together. He offered formative feedback at the end of class and asked the students about their learning progress toward the goal and what resources and tools deepened their understanding. To try to make this assignment more relevant, he asked his students to think of a time they had a fight with a friend or parent and to identify three factors that led to this fight. This modeled the process intended for the Civil War. He was surprised that this quick introductory discussion deepened students' understanding of how different sides of the conflict could have different reasons for the fight. This level of discussion had not been evident previously and took the discussion beyond simple memorization of the facts.

- **Plan for variability in recognition networks: Offer options for representation.** Mr. Amber knew there was a range in students' background knowledge about the causes of the Civil War, in the language and vocabulary they had, and in their ability to perceive the information in the lecture. He offered a few more options for representation, including a PowerPoint presentation bulleting key information represented with text and an associated image, a concept map of how the content aligned to previous classes, an annotated current event article that aligned to his lecture, and a related video on the topic. He thought about videotaping the lecture so it could be listened to again by students who were absent, or who wanted to adjust the pace of delivery to hear parts again.

- **Plan for variability in strategic networks: Offer options for action and expression.** Mr. Amber offered a range of strategies students could use to demonstrate understanding of the causes of the Civil War. He offered the option for students to share their notes about the topic with each other; to let students use handwritten notes, computers, recording devices, or other tools to construct their understanding during class; or to have a graphic organizer to help organize the content.

The UDL framework helped Mr. Amber reflect on the strategies he already used, the barriers that were still in this part of the lesson, and new ideas he could integrate into the environment to support learner variability.

Recap, Reflect, and Discuss

The UDL framework offers guidelines to proactively design environments that anticipate variability in recognition networks (options for perception, language, and comprehension), strategic networks (options for physical action, expression and communication, and executive functions), and affective networks (options that recruit interest, sustain effort and persistence, and for self-regulation).

With this in mind, consider the following questions for reflection and discussion:

1. How do the UDL guidelines, options for representation, action and expression, and engagement, help educators intentionally design for predictable variability?

2. How can you shift the language in your classroom to focus on making changes to the design of the environment to reduce barriers, instead of labeling and accommodating learners?

Chapter Summary

Variability is pervasive across the nervous system, whether in the size and connectivity of different parts of the brain, the size of the central and peripheral visual fields, or the density of rods and cones in the retina of the eye. Because we know this variability exists among learners in every context, we must design for it. Just as a "one-size-fits-all" gym will not meet the needs of the members, a "one-size-fits-all" learning experience will not meet the needs of all learners. However, trying to identify and design for all sources of human variability can be overwhelming.

The UDL guidelines offer a systematic and proactive way to design learning experiences based on three identified brain networks involved in learning. Recognition networks are involved in perception, language, and comprehension. Strategic networks specialize in how we physically act, express, and integrate executive function skills such as goal setting and progress monitoring. Affective networks, including the cingulate cortex and amygdala, help recruit interest, sustain effort and persistence, and are involved in self-regulation. They are like the rudders, or guides, for our decision making.

Brain networks are interconnected in unique ways, making each human connectome—including all the connections within the brain and how they relate to functions and behaviors—distinct. Learning is dependent on the interaction between the individual and the environment, and because each person's brain network is unique, we must design intentionally and flexibly for the range of learners. The more we can do this proactively using UDL, the less retrofitting and reteaching we will need to do, and the more inclusive our learning environments will be from the outset.

Revisiting the Educator Dilemma

As related in the anecdote at the start of this chapter, Shakira was told to work with the Level 2 reading group, which was measured to be the appropriate level for her reading. However, this shift disengaged her, and she started reading less. From a UDL perspective, we know there will be predictable variability in the reading skills of any class or group, even within a Level 2 reading group. To address the variability, UDL can be used to design options that align to the intended learning goal and that support the perception of the context. A little flexibility may help the context be appraised as more engaging and ultimately help her progress and gain the necessary reading skills.

Here are some steps a teacher can take:

- **Clarify the goal.** The goal for this lesson was focused on reading comprehension. She really wanted students to be able to share the important details of what happened in the story. How could she also make this goal relevant and meaningful? When in life do students need to be able to share important details of an event? She kicked off the lesson with a short, silent cartoon and asked students to focus on the important details they needed to comprehend the sketch. Note that at another time, the goal may be about decoding or reading pace.

- **Use UDL to proactively design for variability.** Use UDL to reduce barriers that might be preventing students from achieving this goal.

- **Provide options for engagement.** Possibilities could include having the opportunity to select from a few readings or to discuss for comprehension with a peer. Frequent formative feedback on comprehension could be offered. Ideally, educators hold high expectations for all their learners to achieve challenging learning goals.

- **Provide options for representation.** The teacher could offer a digital version of the text that can be adjusted for text size, font, and contrast. The digital version could also enable students to quickly define new vocabulary with a single click or to have

the text read aloud by the computer (because decoding text is
not the goal in *this* lesson).

- **Provide options for action and expression.** Offer preview
  questions before the reading or a checklist of understanding.
  Students could draw or write about their understanding or fill
  in a graphic organizer. These options are directed at building
  comprehension.

Notice that the options outlined here are just suggestions and
are teaching strategies educators already use. What is different about
UDL is that educators are proactively and intentionally integrating
options into the environment that reduce barriers toward the intended
goal and are available for all learners. The options selected are based
on (1) the intended learning goal, (2) resources available in the context, and (3) teacher and student preferences. When the goal changes,
so do the options, and each learning environment will have a unique
set of resources and materials. The strategies suggested here are not
exhaustive but are intended to model how to use the UDL guidelines
to support predictable learner variability toward an identified goal in
any context. How can reflecting on this educator dilemma inform your
design for an upcoming learning experience?

Teacher Connection: UDL Application in the Disciplines

In the following examples, notice how different disciplines incorporate the UDL guidelines by having options for representation,
action and expression, and engagement in alignment with the
intended goal. Although many of the strategies are not new, the
approach to proactive, intentional design that aligns to the three
learning brain networks and is available for all learners is often
different from traditional lesson design that differentiates, modifies,
or accommodates.

Gym Class Example

Goal: To improve cardiovascular fitness by keeping your heart rate elevated for 15 minutes.

Why: Cardiovascular fitness helps prevent heart attacks and promotes a lifetime of healthy habits.

Traditional Lesson: Students all run a mile, and the teacher notes that there are usually barriers in engagement and effort.

Options for Representation: Students can choose how to gain background information about how to measure heart rate, through either a teacher explanation or a video.

Options for Action and Expression: Students can choose to jog, power-walk, or play a game of tag for 15 minutes, with frequent heart-rate checks.

Options for Engagement: Students jogging or walking can listen to music on headphones or pace with a friend. They will be given feedback about their cardiovascular fitness through use of heart-rate monitors.

Math Class Example

Goal: To learn how to solve for the variables in the Pythagorean theorem.

Why: The teacher created a scenario where students were building a spiral staircase for a Taylor Swift concert (or another musical artist of students' choice). They need to determine the step measurements using the Pythagorean theorem.

Traditional Lesson: Students complete a series of Pythagorean theorem worksheet problems with classmates. The teacher notes that there are usually barriers in retaining understanding and of using the equation in real-life situations.

Options for Representation: Students are given examples that highlight the key processes and symbols in the equation. Different colors are used for tracking each variable.

Options for Action and Expression: Students have triangles they can manipulate, and they can use calculators. The overarching staircase problem is broken down into subcomponent parts.

Options for Engagement: Students are invited to look for examples around the classroom where they can use the Pythagorean theorem. They work in groups and are given answer keys to check their progress, and the teacher roams from group to group to check for understanding and offer feedback.

Create your own example for applying UDL to your context:

Goal:

Why:

Options for Representation:

Options for Action and Expression:

Options for Engagement:

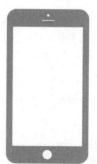

Social Media Connections

#CAST_UDL

#UDLChat

#EndOfAverage

3

FOSTER THE DEVELOPMENT OF BRAIN NETWORKS

Emotional affect can be envisioned as a lens that constantly colors our realities. The lens is so pervasive and ubiquitous that it's easy to forget that it's there . . . the lens is always there, subtly influencing how we see the world.

—Trevor van Gorp and Edie Adams,
Design for Emotion

Brain Research	Design Strategies
• We use all of our brain, even for simple tasks. There is no "learning style" in the brain. • The default mode and "looking-out" networks work together to regulate attention systems. • What we do changes the brain, including myelination, connectivity, and pruning of neurons. • Both nature and nurture contribute to the structure of brain networks.	• Recognize that learning preferences are context-dependent (not neurological constructs). • Integrate reflective and active learning opportunities. • Provide process-based feedback and time for practice. • Incorporate models to build a foundation of expectation.

Educator Dilemma: On the first day of my class, Martha boasted that she was "a natural" at math and science and had always easily earned *A*s in these classes. "I'm a left-brained analytical type." However, I started to notice that in my 11th grade physics class, Martha rarely completed the homework sets and tended to give up quickly, especially on challenging problems. If she is a "math-science" person, why isn't she thriving with these challenging problems? In what ways does this educator dilemma resonate with you?

Learning Styles

Perhaps you've taken some kind of survey to determine your learning style. For example, a question might read "If you could choose a writing assignment, would you rather (a) write a story about a bee that saves the world, or (b) describe the three major rock classifications?" One interpretation of responses is that those who answer (a) are more "right-brained" thinkers—creative and free-spirited as they write a story about a hero bee. Those who answer (b) are more analytical and "left-brained" as they methodically outline and compare the classification of rocks. Popular media supports the notion of "right-" and "left-" brain thinkers with the generalization that the "logical-left" brain is more analytical and attentive to details and the "intuitive-right" brain is more creative and artistic, seeing the "forest over the trees." Studies report that more than 70 percent of classroom teachers believe students to be either right- or left-brained.

However, survey questions such as the example just given can be a challenge to answer. Sometimes you might prefer to write a story about a bee, especially if you had just experienced some kind of activity that captivated your interest, such as watching a video about the bee waggle dance. Perhaps you have access to a graphic organizer that helps to organize the writing of the bee story, and that could drive your selection. A recent visit to a rock exhibit at the local science museum might change your answer completely. The option to brainstorm with a friend who loves rocks might make you more inclined to choose the rock categorization essay. In other words, as noted previously, the context, environment, or options available for the intended goal influence the preference.

Generalizations about learning labels, such as "right brained" or "visual thinker," often do not consider the context or learner variability. They do not consider the plasticity of the brain or its ability to change based on use. In fact, only a very small subset of individuals can actually claim to be "right"- or "left"-brained: those who have had a hemispherectomy. Take for example, the story of Nico. To reduce the frequency of recurrent seizures, Nico had most of the right hemisphere of his brain removed when he was 3 years old and this makes him truly "left-brained." The old, overgeneralized view of the brain as being either right- or left-brained would predict that Nico has significant right-brain deficits, such as reduced creativity or spatial manipulation. However, he showed "no major problems in cognition, sociability, and emotion. . . . I have so far been unable to find a single specific cognitive impairment produced by the right hemispherectomy" (Battro, 2000, p. 53). Nico's story is a remarkable example of brain plasticity, or the ability of the brain to change based on the demands and actions of day-to-day experiences. His left hemisphere was able to build the necessary neural circuits to compensate for a missing right hemisphere. For example, "his drawing by hand is still well behind his spatial cognition. We are currently offering him a wide variety of possibilities and techniques for improving his drawing abilities" (p. 53).

In any moment, a multitude of brain circuits are active in an interconnected symphony of exchange. Even in mundane tasks, no part of the brain has been found to go unused. There are structural specializations within the brain, but isolated regions never act independently. They are interconnected and part of *networks* of brain activity. For example, the *parahippocampal cortex* (PHC) is generally involved in recognizing spatial information, such as the configuration of furniture in a room or the arrangement of buildings along a street. More recent studies show the PHC as part of a *network* of brain regions involved in a host of different activities related to spatial configuration, from imagining plausible chess moves to predicting what comes next in a story. The PHC is even active when recognizing an emotion during a situation, such as identifying the feeling you get when you enter a science classroom or open a social studies book.

The brain imaging technique known as *functional magnetic resonance imaging* (fMRI) shows areas of the brain that "light up" during different situations. When neurons are active, they burn glucose, and the fMRI highlights the *difference* in glucose activity during a very specific task (such as finger tapping). The image is not representative of all of the brain activity at a given moment, because most of the brain is active. The highlighted areas can lead to misunderstandings of the brain as having isolated, localized functionality. However, the brain is never active in just isolated regions or hemispheres, as the name of a particular learning style or label may imply; instead, the brain is active across many networks at every moment. Consider the following list of some of the networks that are activated for the simple task of hearing the word *school*:

- **Auditory networks** perceive sound waves and information about pitch, rhythm, and tempo of the word.
- **Visual networks** associate images we have for school.
- **Phonologic networks** aid in language comprehension.
- **Memory networks** associate the meaning of *school* with past experiences.
- **Emotion networks** associate appraisal (enjoyment or dislike) of school and activate physiology (heart rate, blood pressure, etc.) and cognitive processes (goals, attention).

The Never-Resting Brain

Take a moment and stop reading this book—really! Close your eyes, take some deep breaths, and sit in stillness for a few minutes (if you have a timer, set it for at least three minutes). Notice how your thoughts shift during this time. What did you think about first, in the middle of the time span, and at the end?

The brain is active even when we are idle or daydreaming. A student daydreaming still has a dynamic brain! Studies of "downtime" show evidence of two broad, coordinated brain network systems that are important for different aspects of learning: a "looking-out" network and a "looking-in," or default mode (DM), network. The looking-out system is involved in moments of attention such as perceiving sensory input from the environment, paying attention to the directions for a task, activating motor coordination, executing the steps to complete the assignment, and recalling factual information. It is the one we typically think of when we tell students to "pay attention" and when we envision students in active participation and engaged in productive work. By contrast, the default mode is active during our awake but quiet times, such as moments of self-reflection and imagining. It is active for critical social-emotional learning, such as when we feel empathy (share feelings), weigh a moral dilemma, or feel the effects of someone else's situation.

Both the looking-out and DM systems are critical for us to know about as we think about the greater goals of education that extend beyond content mastery and include developing lifelong learners who contribute to society as just, compassionate citizens. They are critical systems for us to value as we design learning experiences.

There is evidence that both the looking-out and the DM networks are active during infancy and that coordinated patterns develop throughout adolescence. As you likely anticipated, there is also variability in terms of when and how these looking-in/-out systems are activated. The two coregulate each other, so when one is engaged, the other is less active. For example, when I asked you to pause and reflect for a few moments at the start of this section, you likely shifted from the looking-out system you were using to pay attention to reading the text to more of the DM.

How did your thought pattern unfold when you closed your eyes? Often, we begin thinking about external cues and observations, such as something we just saw or heard. Then we often begin to shift inward to monitor our own internal states and being. We begin to reflect on others (along with our place in relation to others) and empathize with the experience of others.

During the course of an academic day, it is important to find a balance in the activation of both systems. At times, we want to engage learners in content, skill, and action components of the looking-out system. In addition, we need to design opportunities for quiet moments to connect, envision, empathize, and ponder the significance and broader implications of what is being learned, activating the DM network. Finding time for quiet reflection can be challenging in large classes with active, collaborative, content-dense goals. As a middle school principal observed, "I think our daily schedule is so rigid and fast-paced that neither students nor teachers pause and take time for reflection." How can we design classroom spaces and curricula for both active and reflective learning opportunities?

Even during quiet moments, many brain networks are active, processing and building connections for learning. Our brains are not isolated organs with segmented functional regions but are interconnected and intertwined with our internal body systems as well as with our external environments, classrooms, and communities.

Recap, Reflect, and Discuss

We use all of our brain, even for simple tasks; there is no generalized "right-brained" or "left-brained" learner. In fact, even when we daydream or reflect quietly, our brains activate default-mode networks that are important for developing social-emotional skills (Immordino-Yang, 2015).

With this in mind, consider the following questions for reflection and discussion:

1. How can you shift language in your classroom away from generalized learning labels to be more about variability and interconnected networks?
2. How can you design your learning environment to address both the "looking-out" attention and default mode (DM) networks?

Brain Plasticity

How big is your friend network? Do you think you could grow your friend network from 2,500 to 15,000 in two years? Could you sustain that many friends over time?

At birth, the brain has billions of neurons, and each can create synapses with as many as 2,500 other neurons—which is a lot of potential connectivity! By age 2 to 3, each neuron increases that connectivity to synapse with an average of 15,000 other neurons. However, by the time we are adults, we may have only half the number of synapses. Why do we lose much of that connectivity? Based on what we do, or the demands and interactions with the environment, the brain adapts and changes. Neurons that are active build synapses, whereas those that are not used are pruned away: we "use it or lose it." This is a remarkable feature of the human brain; we are born with tremendous capacity to learn, and we refine our connections based on our interactions with our environments.

When learning takes place, the brain changes in a few key ways: (1) myelination, (2) connectivity, and (3) pruning. *Myelin* is a fatty substance that surrounds and insulates neurons. Imagine a neuron like a drinking straw. Now imagine trying to drink water through a straw if it has holes in it—it's slow and inefficient. Neurons, like the straw, have channels (like the holes) along their axons that allow chemicals to enter or leave. Myelin "seals" the channels, making the flow of the electrochemical signals faster and more efficient within the neuron. Myelin is like having duct tape around your leaky drinking straw; it helps water move more efficiently as you drink. During new learning, signals are repeatedly fired, which encourages myelination of neurons and results in faster signal transmission. You may have experienced a subtle effect of myelin on your neurons. When you stub your toe, you first feel the touch, which is perceived by fast, myelinated neurons. Then a split second later, you experience the pain, which is perceived by slower, non- or lightly myelinated neurons.

Also during learning, connections between neurons are enlarged and increase so that "neurons that fire together wire together." Density and complexity of dendrites and axons—structures involved in receiving and sending electrochemical signals—become more intricate with use. Imagine this to be like two neighbors building connections. You begin to share resources, perhaps lawnmowers or kitchen supplies, and then maybe keys to each other's homes. When one hosts a party, the other joins, too!

In addition, during learning, there is pruning (removal) of unused neurons. It can seem contradictory to lose neurons when you learn; however, think of this like a good spring cleaning. When you get rid of the extra, unused items cluttering your home, you are able to function more efficiently with the items you do need. You don't have to waste time cleaning or maintaining those unnecessary items. Neurons that are not active wither away, and this is an energy-efficient adaptation.

Learning builds brain networks to be myelinated (faster), more connected, and more energy efficient. These brain changes can take time to establish, and it takes energy to sculpt these changes. When we first start to learn something, the process takes more energy as our brain undergoes these changes. Once we have the background and experience, it takes less energy to do the same tasks. Students who already have experience with a topic will already have established connections, myelinated neurons, and pruning of unnecessary connections. First-year teachers or educators learning a new curriculum or course content—or any of us—will undergo these neurological changes when we learn. Once you have learned something and these signals become robust, you may actually become less flexible to change as pathways and brain processes are more set. It takes energy to continue to grow and change.

Brain changes can take place at any point throughout life. We can always sculpt our brain, although young children experience the most significant changes. In teenage years through the 20s, the frontal lobes undergo their most dramatic developmental growth, contributing to observed changes in goal-directed behavior and personality. The average adult brain grows approximately 700 new neurons a day in the hippocampus alone. This brain plasticity, or the ability of the brain to change, continues throughout life, depending on how we interact with the environment. Even our own thoughts can change our brain.

Where there is a need, the brain directs energy to nourish and grow. For example, individuals who grow up surrounded by spoken language that emphasizes tone, such as Chinese and Vietnamese, have increased connectivity in brain networks involved with tone. If tone is not an important part of our communication, the brain does not expend unnecessary energy developing those brain networks. Although the brain generally does not regenerate damaged or lost nervous tissue, it is able to respond to a dynamic environment. Individuals with stroke damage, for example, are able to remap pathways and connectivity to regain functionality that may have been lost (Hara, 2015). It takes effort and requires work, but the brain is always changing—we can never stop learning! Neuroscientist

Paul Bach-y-Rita, a pioneer in the study of the brain's plasticity, explained the brain's responsiveness with this analogy:

> If you are driving from here to Milwaukee, and the main bridge goes out, first you are paralyzed. Then you take old secondary roads through the farmland. Then, as you use these roads more, you find shorter paths to get where you want to go, and you start to get there faster. (quoted in Doidge, 2007, p. 9)

It can be expected that for any lesson or learning experience, learners will have variability in their neural myelination, connectivity (axons, dendrites, and synapses), and pruning patterns. Some learners have prior background knowledge and experience with a topic and have robust brain-network connectivity, like driving on a smooth, fast highway that supports fuel efficiency. Others may be just forging new neural pathways, like off-roading through dense, unpaved, fuel-demanding terrains. A challenge for educators, who have deep experience in their disciplinary content, may be to recall what it feels like to be a very new learner without background in the subject. We see connections and meaning in the content and even integrate vocabulary seamlessly, and this can be challenging for a new learner. Students who are just learning the basics are activating more brain networks and burning more glucose in order to myelinate and build connections, more so than their experienced peers. It is not that they are less smart—just less experienced. There is variability in background experiences and cultural values that shape our neural networks. We want to value this variability and celebrate and learn from the range of all learners. We can anticipate this neural variability for any content, skill, behavior, or social-emotional component. Therefore, it is essential to design options so new learners are able to build relevant background, be strategic and goal-directed, and be engaged and empowered to take on more complex learning. Here are some suggestions:

- Activate learning with familiar connections so students can build on previous knowledge and skills.

- Offer options that review basic background information, highlight key patterns, and feature important terminology so that new learning has a solid foundation.

- Allow opportunity for practice at different levels so all learners are growing. Those who are more experienced need additional opportunities to learn in service of the target goal.

- Offer flexible options for when and how learners can take "brain breaks." The brain is an energy guzzler that imbibes roughly 20 percent of the body's energy, so options to move, such as stretching, standing, walking, or playing, can increase oxygen intake and help keep the brain fueled with energy. Note that we all do not need breaks at the same time and in the same way. In other words, all students do not need to do 20 jumping jacks for a "brain break." Consider how to incorporate relevant opportunities and flexibility to be active and move within a classroom space or within a learning experience.

Recap, Reflect, and Discuss

The brain changes during learning to be faster (myelinated), more connected (synapses, dendrites and axons), and more efficient by pruning unused neurons. Novices and experts have different types of brain activity.

With this in mind, consider the following questions for reflection and discussion:

1. What is something you have learned to do well that seems to be easy for you now?

2. Recall the process of that learning and the effort and work it took to get to that level of expertise. How can you empathize with your learners and remember what it feels like to be a novice?

3. What strategies can you incorporate into a lesson design to support variability in background experiences? How can you design to anticipate both novice and more experienced learners?

Nature or Nurture: A Brief History

Mozart was composing music by the age of 5; Picasso painted *Science and Charity* when he was 15; and Michelangelo completed his most famous sculptures before he was 30. At age 4, child savant Ettore Majorana could instantly multiply three-digit numbers in his head. How much of a skill for learning is due to innate brain structures (nature), and how much is influenced through our actions and experiences (nurture)? Understanding of the brain and the balance between nature and nurture is a topic that has been debated over time.

Historically, understanding the brain has been challenging because it is deeply encased in the skull. Aristotle claimed the brain was "a radiator for cooling the blood that was overheated by the seething heart. The rational temperament of humans was thus explained by the large cooling capacity of our brain" (Bear, Connors, & Paradiso, 2007, p. 5). Descartes believed the brain to "work like a valve to control the movement of animal spirits through the nerves that inflate the muscles" (p. 7). Trained phrenologists in the 19th century felt protrusions of the skull to proclaim attributes such as cautiousness, secretiveness, suaveness, or even propensity to steal (p. 10).

Individuals who sustained brain damage helped scientists better understand the functionality of different parts of the brain. In the 17th century, Paul Broca observed upon autopsy that damage to the left frontal area of the brain was evident with individuals who had difficulty moving muscles needed for speech. Individuals with damage to this area knew what they wanted to say, but lack of muscle control from the brain damage left them sounding like they were babbling nonsense. In the late 1800s, an accidental explosion sent a tamping iron through the frontal lobe of railroad worker Phineas Gage's brain. He survived the blast, and amazingly, most of his cognitive capacities remained intact, such as memories and visual and auditory processing. However, the frontal-lobe damage affected Gage's personality and his ability to set and follow through with goals. He became less motivated and more profane; "his friends and acquaintances said he was 'no longer Gage'" (O'Driscoll & Leach, 1998, p. 1673). Cases of brain damage such as these led to the emergence of a growing body of evidence for the specialized functionality of different brain regions.

Today, we have the advantage of being able to peer inside the living brain through neuroimaging techniques. We do not have to wait for an autopsy or an extreme accident to infer brain function. This advance helps us to better understand the regional specializations, but most importantly to see how interconnected, variable, and malleable the brain is. These are key pieces to focus on when discussing the brain with students. We now know that we are born with a basic brain structure (nature), but the brain can change based on our interactions with the environment (nurture). For example, neuroimaging enables us to observe an increase in the size and connectivity of finger-movement regions of the brain for musicians who spend lots of time moving their fingers while playing a musical instrument. We know that our brains change based on what we do—a combination of nature and nurture.

Sculpting Brain Networks Through Work, Experience, and Practice

Imagine the brain as a hillside covered with fresh snow. Depending on the context and activity, the snow-covered hill will change. People sledding down the hill, snowshoeing around the perimeter, or cross-country skiing will shift the contours of the snow. Factors such as exposure to the sun or shade, the presence of rocks and trees, or new weather conditions such as freezing rain or hail will further shift the hillside. Some areas become well-paved, smooth runways, while other areas remain unused or melt away. No two hillsides will ever be the same.

Similarly, the brain begins before birth with a foundational "hillside" shape that we inherit from nature. Mozart inherited a basic brain structure. His prolific playing, composing, and feedback from the environment further sculpted his brain. This brain plasticity continues throughout life, although it is generally more flexible at a younger age. This is why something as extreme as a hemispherectomy is typically performed during childhood. You may recall that the right hemispherectomy performed on Nico, the boy mentioned earlier in this chapter, took place when he was 3 years old.

This relationship between age and brain plasticity also explains how certain skills, such as language acquisition, can be easier to develop at a younger age. However, at any age, changes in the brain take place in a relatively short span of time. In a research study (Kauffman, Théoret, & Pascual-Leone, 2002), individuals were blindfolded for five days, so they received no visual input to the brain. Then for hours each day, the participants learned to read Braille, increasing the tactile input to the brain. After this short trial, areas of the visual cortex were recruited for the tactile tasks. When the participants touched the Braille letters, the visual cortex activated. This study shows how quickly the brain can change, how interconnected the brain is, and how the brain can be sculpted through hard work, experiences, and practice.

In the classroom, although we cannot see the changes in our students' brains for ourselves, we know that changes are happening all the time. We can see changes manifest in their actions and skills in what they perceive and comprehend, and in how they persist and engage. We know there will be variability both from differences in inherited brain structures (nature) and experiences (nurture). We should discuss the neural processes of learning with students so they understand how their hard work and effort will change their brains.

One study reported positive outcomes, including reducing the effects of stereotype threat, when students were taught about brain plasticity (Aronson, Fried, & Good, 2002). Specifically, they were taught how the brain builds new connections and faster signals with hard work and practice, known as the incremental theory of intelligence. "Students who were encouraged to view intelligence as malleable reported greater academic engagement and obtained higher grade point averages than their counterparts in two control groups" (Aronson et al., p. 113).

Students can reflect on how their own brain maps change based on the activities they are practicing or working to achieve. One middle school student observed, "When I work hard at a math problem, I think about how I am building my brain and why learning math is important." On the other hand, this comment from a high school teacher acknowledges the consequences of lapses in academic learning: "Thinking about how quickly the brain can change makes me think about our two-month summer vacation—no wonder students do not remember what they learned the previous spring." You can use the snow-covered hillside metaphor or have students draw their own brain map, or homunculus, at different times during the school year to highlight how their effort and hard work is sculpting their brain.

A *homunculus* is a representation of your body as it might be if we could peer inside your brain. It is based on your particular nature-nurture combination. For example, if a student plays a lot of guitar, then motor areas of the fingers will enlarge. If a student practices multiplication tables, then number areas of the brain will expand and become more connected, myelinated, and efficient. It can be powerful for learners to see that individuals are not just "smart" at a skill but have built that skill over years through use. One student commented, "I thought that Sam was just good at math and that I wasn't, but then I saw that he had been doing math at home for years and I understood why he got it faster than I did."

Recap, Reflect, and Discuss

Current understanding of the brain tells us that it is sculpted through both nature and nurture. We are born with a unique foundation (nature) and then change the brain based on what we do (nurture). Brain plasticity can occur throughout our lives and into adulthood. Learning is a result of this interaction of the individual with the environment that changes the brain.

With this in mind, consider the following questions for reflection and discussion:

1. How does the metaphor of the brain as a snow-covered hillside relate to how both nature and nurture sculpt the brain?
2. How can you share with students our understanding of brain plasticity and apply it to learning in your class?

Building the Brain Through Feedback and Highlighting the Learning Process

Emotion is the core of learning, and engagement in learning includes not only interest but also self-regulation and persisting through challenges. What is something you have had to work really hard to learn? How do you acknowledge the process and effort required for learning in your classroom? What if something as simple as how we give feedback to students can improve persistence and lead to subsequent learning? Carol Dweck (2007) did a seminal study about how different kinds of feedback given to students affected behavior and motivation. Half of the students in the study were given process, mastery-oriented feedback that focused on how they were progressing through a puzzle task. For example, the researcher may have commented, "You worked so hard" or "Your strategy to first find the edge pieces worked well." The other half of the students were given fixed feedback that focused on innate qualities of the students, such as "You are so smart at this" or "You are a natural at puzzles." The group with the process-oriented feedback significantly outperformed the fixed-feedback group by as much as 50 percent and chose more challenging subsequent tasks.

Dweck explains how fixed feedback involving attributes such as "smartness" or "cleverness" implies that students are either born with or without a skill—to use our analogy, it is as though their "snow-covered hill" is predetermined and cannot change. She observed that students who had a fixed mindset did not work as hard and generally saw mistakes as negative: "If I am smart, I shouldn't have to work hard" or "If I make a mistake, it means I am not smart." By contrast, process-oriented feedback and a growth mindset encourage students to recognize that mistakes are part of the learning process and that smartness is built through hard work and persistence.

The growth mindset parallels what neuroscience shows about brain plasticity: brain networks grow and strengthen through hard work, experience, and practice. Building a classroom community that values hard work and focuses on the process of learning (growth mindset) can help students feel more comfortable taking on risks and challenges in their learning. Educators can encourage the growth mindset by using the following strategies:

- Offer frequent, specific feedback tied to the learning goal and actions (e.g., not just "good effort" or "nice work," but "When you did this, it helped you make progress toward the goal").
- Make the learning process visible, such as the steps of a math problem or the number of revisions a successful essay underwent. Post and celebrate work-in-process, not just a final perfected product.
- Highlight the different ways students chose to work toward the goal.
- Encourage students to share their learning processes with one another. They can see that we all feel stress or frustration as part of the learning experience and that we all make mistakes in learning.

Imagine that you just read a great novel for a book club, and when you were sharing ideas with friends in the club, you had a riveting discussion. However, the next day when you went to describe the book to a colleague at work, you fumbled with words and did not communicate your ideas well. This can feel frustrating because the night before you had a masterful understanding.

We know that learning is not linear or step-like. Instead, it emerges based on interactions with the environment. According to a proposition known as *skill theory*, learning begins with exploratory sensory and motor actions that help an individual gain insight and consolidate understanding. We listen, try, observe, discover, and explore. From there, and with support of an optimally designed environment, learners build more complex representations and ultimately abstractions of conceptions. In other words, we add layers and dimensions to our understanding. Patterns of EEGs (electroencephalograms) show alignment in the growth of new neural networks as learners advance to the next skill level. What is most powerful about skill theory is how it accounts for the critical role of the interaction of the learner with the environment for the development of the skill. It accounts for how we sometimes seem masterful at a skill but then seem to lose it at other times. Note the rise and fall trends of the optimal skill level. Learning is not something that is mastered and then always present (i.e., learning is not like a step of a staircase). Instead, learning is context dependent: it is strong in some environments but struggling in others. It is like the student who performed a soliloquy in the auditorium but was barely able to get through an oral presentation in my science class.

Over time and with different scaffolds in novel situations, skills build and grow, and learning progresses to deeper levels of mastery (see Figure 3.1).

Skill theory aligns with the Zone of Proximal Development (ZPD) concept described by psychologist Lev Vygotsky. ZPD discusses how

FIGURE 3.1 | Skill Theory

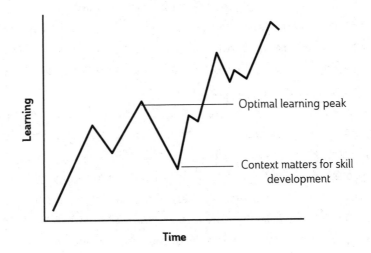

a learner's optimal level can improve with guidance, scaffolds, and encouragement from a skilled educator or peer or by using resources in the environment. Imagine how much more skilled you would be in the book club discussion the next day if you had a note card of key ideas or if you had a friend from the book club with you.

What is empowering about understanding skill theory and ZPD is that we can then think about how to design scaffolds not only as they relate to skills and factual content but also for the construction of social-emotional development. Social and Emotional Learning (SEL) describes knowledge, attitudes, and skills to manage emotions, such as empathy, self-management to set goals and manage stress, or building self-awareness to recognize your own strengths and challenges. We can reflect on the kinds of scaffolds a learner might need to gain these important but often abstract concepts. We can design options in the environment for learners to use as needed in different situations. Educators could integrate Universal Design for Learning strategies (from Chapter 2), such as options for self-regulation or options to foster collaboration. (Note how UDL can provide the "how" and the SEL components are the "what.") For example, how can we design options that scaffold an individual to communicate admiration for a classmate or feel compassion for and reach out to a member of the community who is struggling?

Nature and Nurture at the Cellular and Molecular Levels

What traits do you think you were born with? Are some of us born with compassion or empathy or anger? Which ones can you change? If someone is born with a genetic predisposition for violence, for example, can we actually change that inclination? As noted, both nature and nurture contribute to learning and the brain. Amazingly, we also see this balance at a cellular level, where the inherited DNA (nature) is modified based on our activity (nurture) to change the production of proteins in our brains.

In the early 2000s, neuroscientist James Fallon was studying the neural and genetic patterns of serial killers. He observed that serial killers often have less activity in the orbitofrontal cortex and tend to have the MAO-A "warrior" gene. He concluded that there were significant factors from nature that influenced behaviors and that genes and brain function could determine everything about us (Fallon, 2013). Fallon's conclusion was challenged, however, from surprising facts he learned about his own family history.

Fallon's great-grandfather had been hung for the murder of his great-grandmother, and there were seven other alleged murders in his family lineage. This led him to conduct his own brain scans and examine his own genetic patterns. It turned out that Fallon himself matched the inherited genetic and brain patterns of a serial killer! You might think this finding would deeply concern him or his family;

however, Fallon was missing an important nurture component that was present in most serial killers: he had no history of childhood abuse. He had not demonstrated any kind of propensity for violence. Clearly, nurture plays as intricate and important a role in our brain development as nature.

Even at the molecular level, we can observe that both nature and nurture are at play. We each inherit specific sequences of DNA from our parents. However, over time those sequences of DNA are modified based on influences from the environment, such as aging, diet, chemicals, UV radiation, and stress. Methyl groups ($CH3$) can be added or removed from DNA, changing whether a gene is turned "on" or "off. These epigenetic changes accrue in DNA and can even be passed on to the next generation. For example, a research study examined identical twin mice with matching DNA sequences but that were raised in different environments, with varied diets and exercise options (Fraga et al., 2005). Changes in the expression of their DNA were obvious: one twin was overweight and yellow, while the other twin was thin and brown. The DNA of human identical twins diverges over time as well. Although at conception twins are genetically identical, over time their experiences and environments change their DNA. The difference can be as extreme as one twin having cancer while the other does not.

Although there is still a lot to understand about the relationship between nature and nurture, it is clear that both contribute to learning. Einstein showed incredible genius in his understanding of spatial phenomena and theoretical physics. Autopsies revealed that only a few regions of his brain showed differences, such as the left, inferior parietal area and the ratio of glial cells (helper cells) to neural cells (Diamond, Scheibel, Murphy, & Harvey, 1985; Falk, 2009). However, it is impossible to know for sure whether he was born with these differences or if they were constructed over time and with use. Most likely, it was a combination of nature and nurture.

Similarly, students arrive to a classroom with a foundational "snow hill" of knowledge and experience. By the time they are in middle school, they have had years of experiences that have influenced the development of their brain networks. What we design in our learning environment plays a significant role in sculpting each learner's brain to build not only their content and disciplinary skills but also their social-emotional development. Emotion is essential for learning in the sense that it activates our physiology and engages our sensory systems and cognitive processes. When we integrate options in our lessons for personal relevance, choice, and collaboration; share mastery-oriented feedback; and promote beliefs and expectation that optimize motivation, we help learners sculpt robust neural networks that will enable them to transfer their learning and social-emotional skills beyond the walls of our classrooms.

Recap, Reflect, and Discuss

Both nature and nurture influence learning, at both a neural and a genetic level. How we design learning experiences fosters the development of brain networks, so it is critical that we are deliberate with our target goals, skills, and social-emotional learning we want our students to gain.

With this in mind, consider the following questions for reflection and discussion:

1. How can you include details about the learning brain in your interactions and conversations with students?
2. How can you enhance process-based, frequent, and formative feedback toward the learning goal?
3. What are key emotional skills you will scaffold in the design of your learning environments?

Chapter Summary

Neuroscience shows there is no such thing as a simple right- or left-brained learner. Instead, the brain is incredibly dynamic, with multiple interconnected networks engaged. For example, we have active looking-out networks during tasks that require attention, but we also have default mode (DM) networks that activate during times of quiet reflection and introspection. The brain has the remarkable ability to change based on what we do. We are born with a foundation of brain networks, and we modify those based on how we interact with the environment. Neural changes that occur during learning include (1) myelination, (2) connectivity at the synapses, dendrites, and axons, and (3) pruning, which removes unused neurons. These processes shape brain networks to be like fast, smooth, well-traveled highways.

As we learn, we build new networks and connections. We can design to support learners to build their brains through offering process-based feedback and scaffolding for increasingly complex levels of skills (skill theory and ZPD). The foundational understanding of brain plasticity inspires purposeful design to support variability. We know every learner's brain is constantly being sculpted. We can design to support not only skills and disciplinary content but also behaviors and social-emotional components that are essential for developing empathetic, self-aware, goal-driven citizens.

Revisiting the Educator Dilemma

Let's return to the case example at the start of this chapter, in which Martha struggles to put forth effort for challenging physics problems. Although she may not be aware of it, Martha's view of her intelligence as "natural" for math and science is a fixed mindset. Therefore, she may perceive that hard work is a sign of her not being smart. Instead, through the routines and culture in the classroom, Martha's teacher can give feedback about the process and have the focus be on the work and the effort. Martha can be shown how her brain is malleable and builds myelin, creates new connections, and prunes parts that are not used. These processes lead to learning, and hopefully Martha will gain a deeper understanding of her own strengths and social-emotional skills through the different options available for her to use in the environment. Her brain will remap and build new connections through her hard work.

How can you make connections from this chapter to your own teaching? Here are some ideas for how to support Martha (and all students):

- **Highlight the key steps** for the physics problems, a gesture that may become especially helpful as the problems get more challenging. This support directs and builds foundational neural connections that are necessary to build more abstract concepts and skill development (skill theory).

- **Provide practice problems** that are gradually more complex, and offer frequent, process-based feedback focused on the key steps for solving the problems. Have her choose problem sets that are most helpful to her so she can learn when she needs different scaffolds.

- **Offer real-world, relevant problems** and invite students to work on examples related to their interests. Engage the brain's emotion networks. Reflect on how you can connect to or relate to issues from the school or greater community.

- **Have opportunities for diverse groups to share** how they prepare, challenges they face, and strategies to help overcome barriers so all students see that hard work and effort are necessary. No one is born knowing how to do physics!

This example highlights a math/science course, but these suggestions could be used in any course or with any age. Emphasize the learning process, and provide process-based feedback to help build robust brain networks for desired skills and social-emotional development.

Teacher Connection: 3rd Grade

A 3rd grade teacher describes, "I teach students that their brain changes with use and that it withers without use through a seed analogy that enables students to reflect on their process for building their learning for each unit.

"All seeds have the potential to become flowers. Depending on the soil, light, water, and other flowers and organisms nearby, the seed can flourish and grow or wither and wilt. I tell students they are like the seeds, and we build out this metaphor throughout our unit as a way for them to reflect on their learning. At the start of each unit, I clarify the target goal for our learning, and we record that goal in the sun so students know where they are aiming to 'grow.' Throughout the process, students record what tools and resources best helped them during their learning (these are recorded as the ever-growing stem and leaves). We can have clouds that block the sun and are labeled as challenges that may slow our learning process. However, the challenges (clouds) lead to rain, which in turn helps the flowers grow. I ask students to put reasons they might care about this unit in the soil, as part of the background experience they have to help grow their learning. Having this visual representation of the learning process prompts open dialogue about it."

Social Media Connections

@Brainology
@MindsetWorks
#GrowthMindset
#SEL4MA

4

CAPTIVATE ATTENTION

The effects of emotion directly influence the way we perceive our everyday lives, affecting how we categorize information, make decisions, evaluate risks, and solve problems.

—Alice Isen, in "Dalgleish and Power,"
Handbook of Cognition and Emotion

Brain Research	Design Strategies
Emotion networks dominate perception and cognition.	• Reframe tasks. • Make it relevant.
Background and expectation influence perception.	• Establish routines and patterns for learning. • Contextualize information. • Have high expectations for all.
Novelty attracts attention.	• Change it up in service of the learning goal. • Integrate autonomy and choice, and build to agency.

Educator Dilemma: An 8th grade history teacher reports that one of his students, Manny, "is generally uninterested and often visibly annoyed during my class—and his low grades are not improving." Manny has actually told this teacher, "I know you don't like me, and I don't care if I get a zero on the group work." The teacher says Manny "is often the only one during group work time who does not complete the assignments, and he also does not put forth effort on his independent assignments or homework. His body language suggests disinterest—almost disgust—and he often requests to leave class to get water or to use the restroom. Manny's affect has subtle but observable effects on other students in the class. I hate to say it, but it is easier when Manny is not in class." The frustrated teacher asks, "How can I try to change this downward spiral, let him know that I like him, and engage him in some learning?" In what ways does this educator dilemma resonate with you?

Emotion and Perception

Imagine you come across an "imposter" who looks and acts exactly like a loved one of yours, such as your partner, child, or parent. As much as this individual has the exact appearance and candor of your loved one, you know for certain that this is not the person you know. Your visual networks recognize the physical features, such as the color and style of hair, sparkle of the eye, shape of the cheek bone, and curve of the shoulders, but your emotion networks do not feel the corresponding feelings usually associated with your loved one. Something seems wrong emotionally, and the conclusion your nervous system makes is that this person must be an imposter.

For someone with Capgras delusion, the "imposter syndrome" just described, connections between the visual and emotion networks of the brain are damaged. The feelings that should accompany the visual input of your loved one are absent. So even though it makes no logical sense, your brain concocts this imposter story. When your nervous system receives conflicting signals such as this, the emotional networks dominate.

Emotions drive how we perceive aspects of our environment. For example, on days when we feel negative, an incline can be perceived to be steeper or a building balcony higher than on a day when we feel more positive. In classrooms, emotions influence a learner's perception of a task, the resources available, and even a teacher's intent. For example, a student commented, "I'm not good at math, and neither are my parents. I can't do this assignment; my teacher hates me and there is nothing in class to help me." When the teacher was asked about this student's comment, she noted, "Of course I like [this student] and want her to thrive in my class. There are multiple options for students to use, including extra help sessions, review sheets, and online videos that show how to do the problems. This student does not use any of them." Note that a teacher's perception of students—as illustrated by this example—is also subject to similar influences of emotion.

Negative emotions can taint perception, motivation, and subsequent learning. Students as young as kindergarten arrive to school with self-identified perceptions of their skills: "I'm the only one who needed help with my words; I stink at reading." By middle or high school, students have had years of experience being successful—or unsuccessful—in different subjects: "I'm always in the lowest math group," or "I read two grades below average," or "I love history but I have never been good at writing so I can't major in it in college."

Shifting Perception by Reframing the Task

Because emotions are so powerful, it can be a challenge to shift learners' perceptions and beliefs about their own learning. Reframing tasks can be a way to begin. Before a high-stakes test, the following statement was read aloud to half of the students in a group: "You may be feeling some anxiety. Research indicates that a little anxiety actually helps you to do well on the GRE." The students who heard this prompt before they took the standardized test statistically outperformed the group that did not hear this statement. The only difference between the two groups was this brief comment, yet there was a measurable cognitive impact. The "magic" of the statement was that it reframed a negative emotion, anxiety, in a productive way. Instead of having a racing heart and sweaty palms indicate nervousness and doom, the statement offered a positive affirmation that these feelings were helpful for success. A more positive emotional appraisal of the situation led to improved cognitive performance. At the core of cognition is emotion.

In a classroom, you can use similar subtle but effective reframing strategies that can help shift learners' perceptions of the context. Here are some examples:

- Have students write a self-affirmation paragraph with five items they are good at and care about. This activity helps them see that they are multidimensional, and it can help buffer the effects of a single negative expectation. This kind of self-affirmation has been shown to have lasting positive impact on learning outcomes, including the achievement gap.

- Have consistent, high expectations for every learner, and ensure each that you are confident that they can use the necessary resources available to them to achieve those high goals. This kind of feedback has been shown to positively affect student effort and motivation.

- Offer positive role models from a range of backgrounds in diverse settings that represent the learners in your community and classroom. This helps students to see themselves in varied and potentially novel ways.

Recap, Reflect, and Discuss

Emotions dominate perception and influence motivation and cognition. Reframing tasks, providing diverse role models, and sharing confidence that students can achieve the tasks at hand through hard work and available resources can help shift learners' perceptions of their skills and abilities.

With this in mind, consider the following questions for reflection and discussion:

1. The condition known as Capgras delusion results from damage between the emotion and visual centers of the brain, so individuals think that a loved one is an "imposter." How does this extreme example highlight the importance of emotion on perception?

2. What preconceived expectations do you think learners have about your classroom or subject? How can you influence those perceptions through reframing tasks, sharing high expectations, and providing diverse role models?

3. How do you think your emotions influence your perception of your students or of different classes you teach?

Background and Expectation as Drivers of Attention

What animal do you see in the image in Figure 4.1? If you had seen a similar drawing before, then you had previous background and experience to know which features to look for in both the duck and the rabbit. If you had been prompted with some expectation about

FIGURE 4.1 | **Example of an Optical Illusion**

what animal to look for, then you may have been able to be more strategic in paying attention to relevant details in the image, such as the beak of the duck or the ears of the rabbit. Had the image been contextualized, such as within a pond or in the grass, that context would have influenced your perception.

As an educator, I used to think of attention as something that I had to "grab" or "hook." However, attention is actually a two-way street. Sensory information from the environment, such as my "hook," can get captured by attention networks in the brain of the learner. In addition, and probably more important, previous experiences and expectations of the learner will determine what information is selected from the environment for attention. The two-way street includes the learner and his or her background experiences and emotions, as well as the stimulus in the environment. Consider the following example. White lumps in a PET scan of the lungs can be screened as an indicator of cancer. Take a close look at Figure 4.2 to see if you can find any abnormal white lumps.

You have been primed to know that the relevant information in the image is in the white shapes; therefore, your brain focuses attention there. Processing every detail would expend too much energy, so the nervous system directs attention toward the goal. A study found that radiologists trained to screen for cancerous white lumps in PET scans often did not see the image of the gorilla inserted within the lungs because the gorilla was black, which was not the goal for the screening task. Did you see the gorilla? Approximately one-third of those who look at the image do not. Your brain followed a strategic course by not paying attention to the gorilla, because a gorilla was not related to the goal of locating unusual white lumps. Had you been primed with the expectation of the gorilla or had seen this study before, you probably saw the gorilla this time and you will see it again in the future. Experience and expectation matter.

FIGURE 4.2 | PET Scan of Lungs

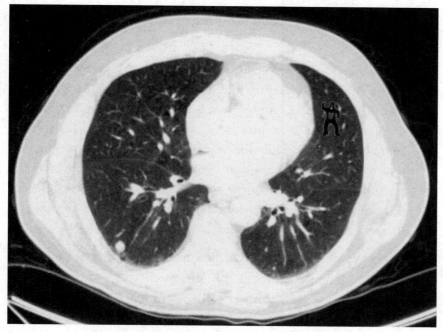

Source: From "The Invisible Gorilla Strikes Again: Sustained Inattentional Blindness in Expert Observers," by T. Drew, M.L.H. Vo, and J.M. Wolfe, 2013, *Psychological Science, 24*(9), pp. 1848-1853. Copyright 2013 by SAGE Publications Inc. Reprinted with permission.

Using Clear Goals to Direct Attention

When we perceive a stimulus, we may then attend to it. Attention can be thought of as a sort of spotlight. With a target goal, whether it is a learning goal set by the teacher or an internal goal the student has, the brain is strategic in how it directs its attention spotlight. If the goal is not clear, attention may be inappropriately focused— more like a wandering searchlight. In addition, a student's goal may differ from the teachers' goal. For example, a student may have the goal of being funny for her peers, which may be quite different from a teacher's goal of having an academic discussion. Another example would be a 5th grade student who is proud of his edible gingerbread house. When asked what makes his gingerbread house so special, the child responds, "The teacher said we got to eat whatever candy was on our house." This child is quite goal driven; however, his goal does not match the teacher's goal for the building project.

> With hocked gems financing him, our hero bravely defied all scornful laughter that tried to deceive his scheme. "Your eyes deceive," he had said. "An egg, not a table, correctly typifies this unexplored planet." Now three sturdy sisters sought proof. Forging along, sometimes through calm vastness, yet more often over very turbulent peaks and valleys, days became weeks as many doubters spread fearful rumors about the edge. At last from nowhere, welcome winged creatures appeared, signifying momentous success. (Ornstein, 1992, p. 187)

How do you make meaning of this story? The content may seem to be a combination of random, disconnected facts. A little struggle and puzzle may be part of the teacher's intent. However, had you initially been told the story is about Christopher Columbus (contextualizing) or been given a few details to focus on for meaning (clarifying expectations), or if you had already been familiar with this story (prior background experience), your attention "spotlight" would be more strategic in focusing on key ideas and ignoring superfluous information.

Contextualizing information, or providing details for what came before or after, or sharing where an idea came from can help students direct attention. Many times in learning experiences, students do not have sufficient background experience to contextualize relevant information in readings, problems, or activities. They may just be memorizing isolated facts, without gaining a greater understanding of the relationships that are important to gain deeper comprehension.

In classrooms, often students who seem "smart" about a topic have had prior background experiences with content, through a parent or tutor or an extracurricular experience; or they may have had clear expectations and an opportunity to contextualize the information to help them direct attention. They may care about the topic. A danger for educators to be aware of is that students who lack related background experiences or context may seem less skilled, lacking focus, inattentive, or, even worse, less smart.

As educators, we want to help build background experiences and direct attention by making sure that pertinent information is perceived, understood, and ultimately learned. Therefore, we need to make the goals and salient features pop. We need to contextualize facts and details and share stories that bring subjects to life and real-world examples to bring a deeper level of understanding and meaning to the situation. Here are a few strategies:

- Model with examples and nonexamples.
- Offer focus questions, annotate articles, include concept maps, and summarize.
- Offer time for practice and reflection in a variety of ways.
- Build and layer content through stories—even factual information has an associated story.

Engaging for Attention

Just because a topic is of interest to you does not mean it will be meaningful for your students. Engagement strongly drives perception; therefore, we must work with learners to make content meaningful and authentic. We pay attention to what matters to us. A high school English teacher knew her students were not engaged in the upcoming lesson on noun-verb agreement. It was not deemed relevant or interesting, and test data showed students did not have this skill. The teacher reframed the traditional worksheet to be a car accident report claim that students needed to fill out (with correct noun-verb agreement) in order to win a hypothetical accident settlement. They watched and simulated car accidents. Because most of the students were new drivers, they understood the relevance of the goal and were much more engaged in the experience. We need to start planning with engagement first so learners want to build experiences, practice, and make their own meaning of the content that can extend beyond the walls of the classroom (Hall, Meyer, & Rose, 2012). Most of what we perceive is immediately discarded and doesn't reach the brain. However, background experience and emotions help tag important information deemed relevant for higher-order cognitive processing.

One of the first stops in the brain for information that has been attended to is the *reticulating activation system* (RAS). It is located in the brain stem and channels sensory information to the *thalamus*, in the middle of the brain. The thalamus sorts information by function: visual information such as color, texture, and depth goes to visual centers in the *occipital cortex*; auditory information such as pitch, tempo, and sound frequency goes to the *temporal lobes*; and tactile information such as temperature, pressure, and touch goes to the *somatosensory cortex* in the parietal lobe. Chemicals such as acetylcholine alert the brain to pay attention to those tagged details for long-term processing.

As educators, we can be passionate experts in our fields and forget what it can feel like to be a new learner. We may think key details are evident in our lessons, but our learners may be missing "the gorilla." A high school senior made a relevant observation: "When we are just told to 'read and take notes' from a chapter for homework, I never know what is important and I usually just copy parts of the text without thinking."

As we experienced with the gorilla example, sometimes we do not pay attention to something that is right in front of our eyes. For example, do you see a small, dark circle in your current field of view? You should—it's really there! Everyone has a blind spot in each eye that should be visible to us at all times. Because there are no rods or cones where the optic nerve leaves the eye, there is no visual input from this area of the retina. We simply do not pay attention to these black spots; in fact, your brain uses your past experiences, expectations, and the current context to fill in the anticipated missing information about what it thinks should be there. That we see a full visual field every day offers a powerful takeaway for us as educators: experience, expectations, and context directly influence perception. We see what we expect.

Using Novelty to Grab Attention

Classroom routines and predictable contexts and experiences can help guide attention and provide safe and familiar schedules, experiences, and expectations. However, in some cases, routine can lead to diminished attention. Consider another example from the nervous system.

Blood vessels are present throughout your eyes and actually pass in front of your visual field. We should see these blood vessels all the time; however, because they do not change and seemingly have no relevance to our daily activity, our brain literally stops paying attention to them. It would be a waste of energy to pay attention to something so static. Similarly, we stop feeling the clothing on our body or jewelry we wear daily; these become irrelevant details for our nervous system. This type of learning is called *habituation*, and it develops through progressively less neural response to a stimulus that lacks meaning. In our classrooms, we don't want the sound of our voice or the routines of our classroom, for example, to become that consistent stimulus that gets ignored.

In the movie *Dead Poets Society*, the teacher (played by Robin Williams) breaks from the monotonous routine of reading from the textbook and encourages students to instead rip out entire pages.

This dramatic shift from the typical routine offered an element of novelty that was memorable to students. It activated their emotions and grabbed their attention. The event was likely "tagged" by acetylcholine and processed into the RAS, the thalamus, and regions of the cortex for memory.

Establishing routines is important, but, as the *Dead Poets Society* example illustrates, changing it up is also important. From a neurological perspective, novelty attracts attention. Incorporate some humor or experiences into your classroom routines. Instead of just reading and writing about a topic, try to bring it to life. Reconfigure your space, include music, change the lights, bring in new materials or technologies and simulations. One teacher had window markers students could use to create scenes related to what they were studying. Although candy, stars, and stickers can be novel and grab attention, they do not necessarily enrich the learning or motivation, and they do not contextualize or make the information relatable. Ideas for incorporating novelty to your routines to purposefully attract attention and highlight key information include the following:

- Start class with a provoking conversation starter, image, current event, or piece of music related to your topic of the day.

- Invite students to be part of the lesson design for new ideas or to help make relevant connections.

- Highlight key information with unique visual cues (use different colors, font, or images) or with auditory cues (use rhyme, rhythm, alliteration, or story-like intonation).

- Break up lectures with activities that are relevant to the goal. For example, have time for a quick turn-and-talk or incorporate relevant movement opportunities to different parts of the room. Find cartoons or humorous connections to the material.

Recap, Reflect, and Discuss

Attention is a two-way street: it is directed from the brain based on experience, expectation, and emotional relevance, and it is directed by factors in the environment such as novelty. Our brain ignores what lacks meaning (habituation) and perceives what is expected.

With this in mind, consider the following questions for reflection and discussion:

1. How did background experiences, expectations, or emotional relevance influence what you paid attention to in the rabbit-duck optical illusion in Figure 4.1 (p. 79) or the lung-gorilla optical illusion in Figure 4.2 (p. 81)?
2. How do you establish common background experiences, expectations, and emotional connections in your lessons? How do you contextualize content so students build a deeper understanding and meaningful connections?
3. What strategies do you implement to integrate novelty toward learning goals?

Using Autonomy to Engage

We generally like options, as becomes evident when listening to orders in a coffee shop: "I'll have a nonfat-caramel-drizzle espresso," "a double macchiato with whipped cream," "a café latte with whole milk steamed to 90 degrees." Coffee shops not only serve a range of coffees, teas, and hot drinks but also offer different choices to match our goal. On a hot morning, we may want a caffeinated, iced drink, whereas on a cool winter evening we may prefer a decaffeinated, hot tea. We learn how to make appropriate choices based on the situation, background experiences, and our goal.

The coffee shop analogy can be extended to think about transforming traditional classroom lessons. What would it look like if our classrooms began to incorporate more goal-driven options and flexible workspaces? And what if we allowed students more autonomy to make their own learning choices based on the lesson goals and their particular variability? Often students are told what to do in school, and they either comply or do not comply. For example, students may be told what to read, at what level to read, and what content they are expected to know, which can stifle motivation. This comment from a 4th grader is illustrative: "I don't know what I like to read; the teacher always just [tells] me what to read."

Though choice can quickly become overwhelming, an educator can optimize choices available during a lesson so they are relevant to the intended learning target. Teachers can collaborate with students on how to approach a learning task so ultimately learners become metacognitive about what they need and how they best learn. This skill will be invaluable for college and career readiness and life outside school. Sometimes students may not make the best choice during a lesson, but the empowerment associated with making a choice will promote engagement and can deepen their understanding about their own learning strengths, challenges, and needs for improvement. A "menu of options" toward the learning goals can help students become agents of their own learning and intrinsically engaged. It can transform a climate and culture for risk taking and self-reliance.

In the following account, I share how a traditional lesson was transformed into a more "coffee shop" experience that supported high expectations, choice, and student autonomy. The goal of the 50-minute biology block was for students to learn the structures and functions of an animal cell. For years, I ran this class period in a routine way that worked well. I began class with an overview of the key information, including images, a video, and a handout that described the parts of the animal cell. Then I let students work on an analogy comparing each part of the cell to a part of the city of Boston. They filled out a table and drew images. I generally thought the lesson went well; however, many students seemed to just comply and memorize the terms. In fact, some had already learned this information from previous science courses. Those who did not necessarily know the function of specific city buildings in Boston had trouble making connections to the unfamiliar parts of a cell (such as comparing the endoplasmic reticulum of a cell to the city's transportation system). The content was boring for some students who were uninterested in learning more about Boston or the cell. The content also had a lot of vocabulary, both for the cell (such as *lysosome*) and the parts of the city (such as *department of public works*). The lesson required a lot of rote memorization, which challenged some students, and I had not designed to anticipate learner variability.

I made a few simple changes to this lesson structure that yielded a very different experience for students—and for me. First, I shared the intended learning outcome I wanted all students to achieve. Then I shared the resource stations that had been set up in my room and that could be used at any time during the lesson: (1) a graphic organizer, (2) an audio station, (3) a craft/junk table, (4) a computer section, (5) a quiet work area, (6) a collaborative corner, and (7) a content review station. Use of these stations was flexible and available for all students, and I let them decide which combination of resources to use to progress toward the goal. I prepared resources at the stations before students came to class; so the graphic organizer related to the cell was ready to use, the computer station had video examples from the cell unit, the audio station connected to relevant content from our textbook, and the review station had notes, highlighted vocabulary, and a summary from my introduction to the cell. This took more time to prepare on the front end, but it paid off in the long term. Students knew the goal and could select what would help them to progress toward the goal. In addition, this content was part of the biology standard exam students took at the end of the year, and I shared examples so they could also practice multiple-choice questions about the cell parts. As students worked, I roamed the room, checked progress, and guided them to appropriate stations, as necessary.

After making these design adjustments I observed such a different class and outcome! Since students could choose their own analogy for the parts of the cell, they engaged in debates about whether Harry Potter or Hogwarts was more like the nucleus of the cell (this was relevant to them!). Two students did elaborate drawings of their analogy of the Death Star from "Cell-Wars," and this group even added music. A student who had never shared his work before to the class volunteered to show his cell model that he had designed on the computer. A dancer worked independently on a "Gi-cell poster" based on the ballet *Giselle*, a comparison that was authentic and meaningful to her. Two students collaborated to make a mini "Pirates of the Cell-aribbean" model using materials from the craft table. One student I thought would want to partner for the activity instead chose to work on his own using the graphic organizer.

Though the classroom looked less organized, students progressed in their own ways, using different options to reach the goal. My job was to monitor progress, check understanding, deepen connections, and help students think about the learning choices they were making. For the few students who finished very quickly, I was able to encourage them to move to a deeper level of learning with the resources already available in the environment and that was still related to learning about the cell.

However, the most important change in this lesson took place when I started to really think about *why* students needed to learn the structures and functions of the cell. What was the relevant connection, and why should they care? I tried to connect the content directly to their own bodies, since each of the cells in their body had different concentrations of the organelles and affected how *their* organs worked. We talked about why liver cells might have more peroxisomes than other cells, as it needs to break apart alcohol (mention of alcohol with high school students was relevant). This led to more student-driven questions about other organs, such as whether exercising might increase the number of mitochondria in their muscle cells or which organelle might be needed in their kidneys when they drink lots of water. We even discussed some organelle-related diseases that had never been covered in my previous discussions in this unit. Contextualizing the terms within something that mattered to the students led to more interest and higher-level learning outcomes. In the process, I learned more, as well, and I couldn't believe how much more meaningful and rigorous the lesson had become.

Not only did students make connections to the content, but they performed well on the final assessment. In fact, the average test grade was higher than it had been in all previous years, and I noticed more reference to cell structures in class discussions throughout the semester. A student even brought in a newspaper article months later, wanting to discuss liver cell regeneration!

I had always offered choices in my lessons, but in this case I integrated a clear, high-level expectation for all students and autonomy to make choices to achieve that goal from the options available. I began to look for additional ways to incorporate choice, relevance, and authentic examples to contextualize the information. I began to let students have more control over their choices, and I used the UDL guidelines to think about how I supported variability by having options for representation, action and expression, and engagement in the materials and methods offered at my stations. Sometimes I thought students didn't always make the best learning choices; however, the process of having them experience the outcome of poor learning choices was valuable in itself. Sometimes I did not know the answers, but I modeled how we could use resources to find the answers, and this contributed to building a classroom that valued the learning process over rote memorized content. How do you think developing this kind of flexible environment might support variability of student emotions and engagement?

My understanding of brain science gave me more confidence in the rationale behind my lesson design, and my classroom was more abuzz with conversations related to the learning goals—much more like a coffee shop. A colleague asked, "How are you able to have this top student, this struggling student, and this English language learner in the same classroom?" I began to give her a brief overview of my proactive design approach and reframed the learning labels to be about variability.

As this anecdote illustrates, the design was intentional and had clear expectations, with options to support the anticipated range of background experiences, interests, and levels of engagement. All choices directed student attention to relevant information. In addition, having high expectations and allowing students autonomy to make choices enhances a deeper level of engagement for learning. Students had the chance to learn about their own preferences in different contexts: "When I worked with a partner on the review sheet, it helped me fill in the details that I missed in class" or "When I worked with a partner on the review sheet, I was distracted. I would rather use the textbook and work on my own." Having students work in different ways to achieve a goal may seem to lead to a more chaotic learning environment; however, it encourages a deeper, more self-directed learning experience. As one teacher observed, "It looks like controlled chaos in my classroom, but the students are more engaged and are learning much more than when they were all doing the same thing at the same time. I enjoy my classes more and am really getting to know my students better as learners." As for the mistakes that students might make in this environment, a 2nd grader offered this view: "It's OK to make mistakes. That's how you learn."

Here's an example that shows how this thinking can extend beyond classroom contexts. My family and I hiked a 13,000-foot mountain one day. Reaching the summit was the goal, and we wanted to achieve it before the predicted late-afternoon rainstorms. We could see the summit from the ground, and we talked about our options. We shared the different strategies we each had for the hike. My son likes to go fast and work on his own. My daughter does not like heights; she wanted to use the paths, take her time, and enjoy frequent snack breaks. My mother wanted to collect a variety of wildflowers, and my sister needed to be sure her puppy could make the climb. Even though we each had different hiking backgrounds, skills, and interests, we were equipped with maps, communication tools, snacks, and options to work together. We each took our own approach up the mountain, adjusting as needed and progressing toward the goal.

Along the way, we shared our progress or noted challenges, such as a very slippery ledge. I had to reconsider my strategies when it became clear that I was feeling the effects of the altitude. My son ascended too quickly and got an altitude headache (he had never had one before). We discussed how his pace, water intake, or training before the hike could be different next time. We all enjoyed the day, felt success and challenge in the process, and shared our experiences. If we all had hiked in the same way, we would have risked losing motivation and a sense of ownership over the experience. We each learned more about our own strengths and challenges and how the options available could support us each as needed. We each had a level of autonomy, or independence, toward achieving high expectations. How can this example be transferred to the design of learning experiences?

Often, our curricular materials are designed for the same learning to occur for all individuals at the same time and in the same way. We know that this is not how the nervous system works. The following are some strategies we can use to align our curricular materials to support choice, autonomy, and high expectations:

- Clearly communicate consistent, high-level expectations for all learners from the beginning of the experience—importantly, the belief that all can achieve them. Unfortunately, we frequently hear educators say, "I didn't think *that* student could do that."

- Share a learning menu or "buffet" of strategies learners can choose to use as they progress. For example, UDL can inform the buffet with options for engagement, representation, and action and expression. If the goal is the target, then there should be no "easy" choice within that learning menu.

- Allow students to make learning choices. Be sure to celebrate successes and mistakes that help them learn more about themselves as learners. Sometimes, a student may not make the best choice, but this provides an invaluable opportunity for learning. For example, a student had not completed the lesson goal and told her teacher, "I should have used that graphic organizer to help me write." As this feedback came from the student herself, she felt more ownership over the experience.

- Contextualize information so students are not working with isolated facts. Continue to work to make connections to real-world applications.

Recap, Reflect, and Discuss

Giving students autonomy to make learning choices toward achieving a high-level, relevant learning goal can enhance engagement for learning. It can take longer to design up front, but it deepens the engagement for learning.

With this in mind, consider the following questions for reflection and discussion:

1. In what ways do you encourage autonomy for learners to make choices in your design toward targeted goals?
2. Try offering one additional option for learners to use toward a goal. What do you observe that is different related to engagement? How did this reduce a learning barrier?
3. How do the strategies in this chapter empower all of the learners in your class-room to engage in the learning process?

Chapter Summary

We have learned from individuals with damage to their brains' emotion networks, such as those with a condition called Capgras delusion, that emotions dominate. They influence perception and "paint" our experiences. Most sensory information from the environment does not make it to the brain; the brain would waste energy if it sorted through every perceptual input. However, engagement "tags" information to be processed and sorted in higher-order cognitive networks for learning.

Educators can help purposefully direct student attention to pertinent information through strategies such as having established routines, highlighting expectations and key background information, and introducing novelty into the mix. We can help students to reappraise a situation toward a learning task and offer consistent, high-level expectations combined with some choice and autonomy to increase student engagement and direct attention for purposeful, meaningful learning. Focus first on designing so the target is relevant, contextualized, and meaningful.

Recall that emotions activate changes in the brain and body physiology that are drivers for learning, such as how we engage, pay attention, and act in an experience. Emotions are tied to predictions that the brain makes about how much energy it will need to expend in that context, based on previous experiences. Often, learners have constructed years of negative emotions associated with learning in classroom contexts. It may take a lot of effort to actively reconstruct these appraisals so learners shift the perception of the contexts to get to engagement with—and perhaps even eventually a love for—learning.

Revisiting the Educator Dilemma

Returning to the educator dilemma at the start of this chapter, recall that Manny's perception of his history class is likely influencing his attention and, ultimately, his learning. If he perceives that the teacher does not like him, that he does not have resources to do the work, or that he is generally not good at this work, those perceptions will drive how he pays attention to events in the classroom.

Here are a few ideas this educator decided to try for an activity, using the concepts from this chapter:

- **Have clear expectations** for the activity so students know the purpose, what they need to accomplish, and why it matters. Try to have the same challenging goals for all learners.

- **Establish clear routines** that students come to expect, such as a warm-up activity ("do now") and an exit ticket, resource centers, a quiet work space, and a collaborative corner.

- **Where possible, offer choice.** Try to be a "yes" teacher, as long as it ties to the goal. For example, Manny asked if he could do his work under the desk to get rid of the distractions of his peers, and it was the most effective work he had done all semester.

- **Introduce an element of novelty** by having a new technology students may not have seen before. Tie it to the learning goal so the novelty is relevant. Work to have real-life connections to contextualize and make the content meaningful. Ask students where the meaning or connection might be.

Teacher Connection: AP Chemistry

Sometimes options can be overwhelming. Sometimes students do not like options: "I prefer when the teacher tells us what to do and shows us how to do it." Advanced Placement (AP) courses often have so much material that students need to get through that educators feel they must resort to delivering massive amounts of information in a "one-size-fits-all" way. What follows is a description from an AP Chemistry teacher.

"I tried offering options other than my lecture for students to learn the content, but they hated the change. When I asked them why, I had really reflective answers! Students did not know what to focus on—they didn't know what was important or relevant (they lacked the relevant background), so they did not know how to make a choice for their learning. The situation was like being asked which restaurant you want to go to without knowing anything about the restaurants or who you are eating with. That lack of knowledge makes it hard to choose! Once I shared the goal and some essential background information, then I was able to offer them two choices about how they wanted to build their understanding and two choices about how they wanted to show their understanding. Now students felt better equipped to make a choice, and they engaged in the learning more purposefully."

The point is to offer relevant options—with enough background to help drive students' attention and choice. Just doing what we are told to do is compliance. Ultimately, we want to build independent learners who are engaged, strategic, and motivated to make connections and become self-aware, compassionate learners and contributors.

Social Media Connections

@cbcUPF
@TEDTalks
www.ted.com/talks/vilayanur_
ramachandran_on_your_mind

5

SCAFFOLD MEMORY

All design is emotional design. Emotion dominates decision making, commands attention and enhances some memories while minimizing others.

—Byron Reeves and Clifford Nass,
The Media Equation

Brain Research	Design Strategies
• We all have some level of *synesthesia*, or connectivity between sensory brain regions, where stimulating one sense leads to an automatic experience in another. • Working memory can be divided into the visual sketchpad, the phonological loop, and the central executive. • Cognitive load limits our capacity to take in more information.	• Offer multisensory options. • Rehearse, discuss, and share. • Organize and make connections clear. • Offer ways to offload information that is being held in mind.

Educator Dilemma: Jeff seemed to be paying attention to my science demonstration, but when it was his turn to do the activity, he had no idea what to do. He completed the first task but seemed lost and confused for the rest of the lab. He tried to copy what other students were doing, but this frustrated his peers. Jeff always seemed to be the one who did not remember what to do, and he appeared quite clumsy in most activities. Was this a lack of motivation or engagement, or could he really not do the work? In what ways does this educator dilemma resonate with you?

Memory Challenge

Throughout parts of this chapter, you will need to remember the following sequence of numbers. Take a minute to commit them to memory:
6, 3, 9, 5, 0, 8, 7, 1, 4, 2, 9, 4.

Incredible Memory

Daniel Tammet made international news in 2004 when he recited pi to 22,514 places. He listed number after number and kept his exact place within the expansive sequence, even with restroom stops, stretch breaks, and an attentive room of media reviewers. When asked how he was able to recall so many numbers, Daniel described a detailed emotional landscape where the numbers were filled with colors, shapes, textures, and personalities.

"Numbers are my friends, and they are always around me. Each one is unique and has its own personality. The number 11 is friendly and 5 is loud, whereas 4 is both shy and quiet—it's my favorite number, perhaps because it reminds me of myself. Some are big—23, 667, 1, 179—while others are small: 6, 13, 581. Some are beautiful, like 333, and some are ugly, like 289. To me, every number is special" (Tammet, 2006, p. 2). Daniel can remember and manipulate incredible amounts of mathematical information, in feats that seem impossible to many. For instance, he can multiply multiple digits, such as 53 × 131, in his head by visually crafting relationships between different numbers in a three-dimensional, meaningful way.

Another memory savant was Solomon, described in the book *The Mind of the Mnemonist* (Luria, 1968). Solomon's memory was so robust that he had to actively work to *not* remember superfluous information. For instance, he would take memorized word lists and burn them in a desperate attempt to get rid of the indelible memory. Solomon could remember detailed strings of items from 15 years earlier, and, like Daniel, he had enriched sensory and emotional number associations. He described numbers as having gender, emotion, and size:

> Take the number 1. This is a proud, well-built man; 2 is a high-spirited woman; 3 a gloomy person; 6 a man with a swollen foot; 7 a man with a moustache; 8 a very stout woman—a sack within a sack. As for the number 87, what I see is a fat woman and a man twirling his moustache. (Luria, 1968, p. 31)

Is there something neurologically different for individuals with such robust memory? Can anyone build superior memory skills through hard work and practice? Did you connect emotion, personality, or size to your memory challenge?

Connecting Through Multiple Senses

Sharp cheese, loud shirts, and quiet lemonade. We know what these phrases mean, even though we know their literal meaning does not make sense: cheese does not feel sharp, shirts are not loud, and lemonade is weak or watered down but not quiet. However, these phrases connote meaning. They blend two of our senses together in a way that we understand because our brain networks are heavily interconnected. I had a student once who saw letters as colors, and she described how the word *the* looked like different shades of green, purple, and red.

Synesthesia is a condition characterized by hyper-connectivity between sensory areas of the brain. The dense connections enable one sense to be activated in an automatic, involuntary experience when the other sense is stimulated. For example, "sharp cheese" connects tactile (touch) sense with gustatory (taste) sense. Some-one with hyper-connectivity between auditory (hearing) and visual (seeing) areas of the brain may hear the musical note A-sharp and see an associated color. The most common kind of synesthesia is grapheme-color, in which individuals see letters with specific colors. For example, a *K* might be a shade of blue-green, and an *S* more of a yellowish brown. The dense connections between visual and letter-recognition areas of the brain lead to these perceptual connections. To some extent, we all have synesthesia because our brain networks are very interconnected. Metaphors such as "a heart of stone" or "fit as a fiddle" connect seemingly unrelated items in comprehensible ways, offering evidence of the interconnectivity of our brain networks.

As you may have guessed, there is variability in the connectivity between brain regions from one person to another. More connec-tions are not necessarily an advantage; it depends on the context. Studies of autism, for example, show hyperconnectivity between several brain areas, including areas that integrate information from the environment with information about internal body states. This hyperconnectivity may partly explain sensory-integration challenges in which sounds or visual experiences become overwhelming and intolerable, but in a different context the hyperconnectivity may lead to an increased skill. For example, a student may be overwhelmed by the noises and inputs of a classroom, but then be incredibly atten-tive and tuned in to a specific book, activity, or discussion. Although autism has both hypo- and hyperconnectivity across many brain regions, the key points to remember are that there will be variability and that context matters. No two brains of individuals with autism (or of anyone!) are ever the same.

Because the brain is malleable and can change based on our experiences, we can influence the connectivity by how we interact with the environment. Children who grow up learning tonal languages, such as Vietnamese or Mandarin, tend to have more hyperconnected auditory regions that help distinguish tonal qualities necessary for communication. Two-time memory champion Wang Feng recalled how his memory was not strong growing up, but his persistence and hard work in training more than five hours a day helped him build his memory. Feng describes how he trained for the Deck of Cards challenge by using visual and emotional stories. He imagined the 52 cards in a set location around his house and connected the item to an emotionally relevant story. Perhaps the queen of hearts was a high-heeled shoe located under his bed and the jack of spades a razor on the bathroom sink, and he crafted a story to connect the meaning of the items.

Because the brain is highly interconnected, if we learn information in more than one way, then we build multiple neural pathways. Learning is more interconnected and accessible through these various neural pathways.

Emotion and Memory

Emotions are essential for memory. We are more likely to remember details from an emotionally charged event, such as September 11, 2001, than from a day that was not emotionally wrought. Studies of classrooms have found that individuals had better recall of events when told through an emotional story than through a nonemotional version. "The dramatic event powers its way through the neural pathways . . . into memory storage, and the associated hitchhiking academic information gets recalled along with it" (Willis, 2006, p. 13). This recall is due to the interconnectivity of emotion networks located alongside strategic, sensory, and memory networks of the brain.

In the classroom, the more information is presented through multiple sensory perceptions (e.g., visual, auditory, tactile), the more likely it will be remembered. However, this may be challenging. For example, a high school Spanish teacher complained, "I have to get through 12 chapters this year for students' AP exam. I don't have time for fun skits or activities; I have to teach content."

Here are a few ideas to consider for classroom application:

- **Personalize mnemonics.** Instead of giving a mnemonic to students, such as the order of operations phrase "Please (parenthesis) Excuse (exponents) My (multiplication) Dear (division) Aunt (addition) Sally (subtraction)," invite students to craft their own memory tricks. Those that are more humorous and personal are more likely to be remembered.

- **Incorporate stories.** Craft developmentally relevant stories to paint emotional scenes that are visual and include verbal tone and rhythm (even conflict). For example, high school students are often interested in social relationships. To learn blood groups, an educator shared a dialogue where different kinds of blood groups (A, AB, O) and their proteins (+ or –) were part of social cliques that stuck together or that repelled each other and fought. Contextualizing abstract or complex topics through familiar scenes can help visualize the interactions.

- **Integrate visual, tactile, kinesthetic, or verbal options to process information.** For example, if the goal is for students to represent data on a bar graph, students could build a model, draw, or use the computer. Imagine how an auditory description of a graph or chart might deepen understanding and make it accessible to someone using a screen reader. Experiencing the multiple representations enables learners to transfer core patterns to novel situations. Remember to not label students as being "visual," "kinesthetic," or another "style" of learner. There will be variability—including within individuals—and that context matters for preferences (see Chapter 2). In addition, each student does not necessarily need to do each kind representation. For example, a history teacher had students write the definition and draw a representation of the term. For some students, the drawing was a barrier and a source of frustration. If the goal is to learn the vocabulary, students can have the option to write the definition and/or draw a representation (the drawing is *not* the goal in this case).

- **Ask students.** Don't assume you know what a learner will like. Ask students how they visualize, could verbalize, or could construct meaning.

Memory Challenge, Part 2

1. Try to recite as many numbers as you can, in sequence, from the Memory Challenge at the beginning of this chapter. How many did you recall (out of 12)?
2. Return to the list of numbers. Try to associate the numbers with a color, size, or story.

Damaged Memory

Although you can use multiple strategies to build memory, the formation of memory can come up against physical limits—and some struggle more than others. Patient H.M. was not able to remember colleagues he had worked with for decades or whether his parents were still alive. Due to intractable epilepsy, H.M. had most of his hippocampus (a key region of the brain involved in memory), amygdala, and surrounding cortex removed in 1953. The operation successfully reduced the symptoms of epilepsy; however, it left H.M. unable to form new memories, a condition called *anterograde amnesia*.

Imagine not remembering if you have eaten dinner, the current year, or the plot of a movie. H.M.'s autobiographical memory of events from his own life before the surgery and his procedural memory remained intact. For example, he still knew what he had done on his 10th birthday, and he could still ride a bicycle, as these both happened before the surgery. However, he would forget how old he was or would not know where he was riding his bike on a particular day because these were new pieces of information that had not been processed to memory.

The hippocampus, a primary area removed from H.M.'s brain, functions to pull relevant memory pieces from different areas of the cortex together to form a coherent memory. Like a "puzzle expert," the hippocampus connects puzzle pieces related to senses and emotions. For example, to remember events such as your 10th birthday party, your hippocampus pulls together visual pieces such as the color of the cake and the sight of a friend, sound pieces such as the "Happy Birthday" song, and emotion pieces such as the happiness associated with receiving a special gift. These event "puzzle pieces" are actively constructed by the hippocampus and are contextualized with current events. Without the hippocampus, H.M.'s memory "puzzle" remained jumbled; but practice helped him rebuild some brain connections and attain new learning, although the learning was not as robust as before the surgery.

This neurological perspective on memory formation may deepen understanding as to why certain classroom strategies support or do not support memory. When we integrate multisensory, relevant, and engaging experiences into learning events, we activate the hippocampus to construct a vivid sensory "puzzle" of memories. More sensory and emotional connections (more "puzzle pieces") enable a more coherent, robust memory. We all fall along a continuum of memory ability, and, depending on the context and background experiences, some are able to effortlessly retain information (nature), whereas others need to work really hard to build memories (nurture). If you are asked to remember the string of 12 letters (the same number as in the memory sequence from the beginning of this chapter) A, B, C, D, E, F, G, H, I, J, K, L, then it is much easier as we have background experiences that give this sequence meaning. We can design experiences that enable all our learners to construct meaningful, relevant, contextualized memories.

Recap, Reflect, and Discuss

Multiple sensory experiences and engagement enhance the brain's memory networks to build more robust connections and lasting memory.

With this in mind, consider the following questions for reflection and discussion:

1. Think of something you remember well. How did you use visual, auditory, kinesthetic, or other sensory inputs to construct this memory?
2. How can you integrate emotion and engagement strategies to enhance memory or procedural skills in your classrooms?

A Deeper Understanding of Memory

Throughout this chapter you have been challenged to hold 12 numbers in mind, even though you are also trying to read the text. This skill relies on your working memory. *Working memory* is the part of our memory system that holds temporary information in mind, even in the face of distractions. A classic example of working memory is trying to remember the phone number of a person of interest, even without the help of your smartphone and with friends and events in the environment distracting you.

School is filled with working-memory demands in every content area, for any age group or any skill. For example, group discussions rely on holding information in mind and constructing a response while someone else is talking. Classroom directions are often given verbally and contain multiple tasks for students to hold in mind as they are working. Students not able to hold the pertinent information in mind may look to their peers or around the room for clues about what they should be doing and may appear as though they have not paid attention. A student may seem disinterested, distracted, or off task, but that may not be the case. The student may actually have an underlying deficit in working memory. "Behavior problems may be related to memory challenges, not due to a lack of interest or lack of caring about schoolwork" (L. T. Rose, personal communication, 2010).

Working memory varies from student to student, and a deficiency can look different depending on the context. For instance, in math class, it may manifest as an incomplete or partial answer to a multistep word problem. Individuals may focus on one part of the problem and lose track of the other parts they also need to answer. In English class, it may seem like poor reading comprehension but may actually be due to not being able to hold in mind what just happened in the story as new information is read. In both cases, the behavior stems from poor working memory. Resources, such as a table to record important information or a separate work space for each part of the problem, can support working memory and allow students to better demonstrate what they know. Imagine a student with poor working memory during a history debate. She may not be able to recall the complete argument, seeming unprepared, even though she had fully researched her case. A simple tool such as a cue card or a graphic organizer can support working memory, allowing her to fully participate as she had prepared.

Sometimes educators are concerned that scaffolds are not available in "the real world" so should not be used in school. The counterargument is that in school, learners should be able to try out and experiment with the tools and strategies that can help them build expertise, highlight their strengths, and support their weaknesses.

Over time, they will need the scaffolds less. You can analyze parts of a lesson through the lens of working memory. Reflect on what information must be held in mind and whether there are ways to "offload" those. For example, having the physics equations available can offload this memory demand so learners can focus on deconstructing the problem. Using a calculator can offload simple computations when the focus is on more complex problem sets. Determine which memory demands are the desired difficulties for the target goal and which can be scaffolded or offloaded in the environment so learners can focus on the desired skill.

"Traffic Control": The Three Components of Working Memory

The following sections dive more deeply into working memory and the connection between brain science and classroom practice. The strategies described can benefit anyone, not just those with poor working memory, and so should be made available to all students. For convenience, working memory is portrayed in terms of three subdivisions: the visual sketchpad, the phonological loop, and the central executive, although current research continues to expand understanding (including the addition of an episodic buffer) beyond these three components. The discussion uses a traffic metaphor: the visual sketchpad and the phonological loop are each like a lane of traffic, and the central executive is like the traffic control officer. Keep in mind that there is variability among learners within each of these subdivisions and even within the same learner at different times. In addition, note that this simple model is limited but can serve to deepen thinking about teaching practices.

The Visual Sketchpad: One Lane of Traffic

A student goes to the whiteboard to write the name of the food he is planning to bring for the class party. In front of the entire class, he writes "dognuts." Laughter erupts and he sheepishly slumps back to his desk, mortified by the silly spelling mistake. He knows how to spell "doughnuts," but in that moment, his ability to hold in mind the spelling and write the word on the board in front of his friends faltered. We have all likely experienced moments like this, where our brain seems to go offline for skills we know we have.

The visual sketchpad of working memory is likely what failed with this student in this moment. It encodes visual information, such as the shapes and sequence of letters in words or the location of objects in space. Even with our eyes closed, we visualize shapes, colors, objects, landscapes, and entire scenes. The visual sketchpad can be thought of like a lane of traffic merging incoming visual information with other sensory information onto a larger "memory highway." As in real life where there is always traffic on the highway, there is always information being processed by the visual sketchpad. In addition, the "traffic" can go both ways; the visual sketchpad is not just idly waiting for incoming sensory information but is actively constructing top-down perception from previous experiences.

In school, the visual sketchpad is always active, when, for example, conducting sequential steps in a lab or other activity, crafting a writing exercise, reading a scene, following directions, or solving a problem. Imagining a character's appearance or actions, visualizing trends shown on a graph, interpreting data, as well as constructing spelling and plot sequences—all of these rely on the visual sketchpad of memory. In the Memory Challenge presented at the beginning of this chapter, you likely used your visual sketchpad to envision the number sequence in your head.

Artist Stephen Wiltshire demonstrates an extreme ability of visual recall. After just a 20-minute helicopter ride over the city of Rome, Stephen sketched a 10-meter panorama of the city that included every precise detail of the entire expanse, including each and every building, street, window, door, and sidewalk. It was as though the incoming visual information was a six-lane superhighway for Stephen, because all the information that entered his visual memory was effortlessly recalled (www.stephenwiltshire.co.uk). On the other end of the spectrum, some individuals struggle to recall even two digits of a phone number or of the Memory Challenge. It is as though their visual sketchpad is a rocky, rutted single lane that allows only one car through at a time.

As discussed earlier, how we interact with the environment influences our visual sketchpad. A research study showed that London taxi drivers had enlarged areas in the back part of their hippocampus where visual sketchpad information is generally stored (Maguire et al., 2000). This enlarged visual sketchpad probably helps them to visualize navigation through the convoluted streets, even with distractions such as roadblocks, blaring radios, or passenger conversations. We are unable to measure whether these taxi drivers were born with an enlarged posterior hippocampus (nature); however, we do know that the years of intense practice and use of the London roadways helped sculpt their brain (nurture). In our classrooms, we can design lessons that help learners build these networks.

Many times, our lessons have unnecessary challenges or barriers in them that are connected to working memory demands. If we make some simple changes to our design, we can reduce some of these barriers so learners are able to focus more on the desired skills of the task. For example, a science teacher gave verbal directions for a lab. She then realized that students had to hold all of the steps she had said out loud in mind while they conducted the lab. It was no wonder she had to repeat herself and reteach so often! Had she also written the information on the board or on a strip of paper, for example, students could reference it when they needed it. This design decision scaffolds the visual sketchpad component of working memory, and by doing so, she helped students keep focus on the desired content-learning skills of the lab. Here are some strategies to support the visual sketchpad component of working memory:

- Provide worked examples so students can visualize expectations, processes, and final outcomes. Having answers or models available in the environment empowers students to seek what they need when they need it and not be dependent on the teacher to pace the learning.

- Offer concept maps or flowcharts to help display key information and relationships.

- Include options to draw, build models, or construct diagrams to enable students to visually manipulate information.

- Celebrate how different representations present the core information. (Note that you do not need to necessarily assess the means, or "how," if the goal is focused on the content.)

The Phonological Loop: A Second Lane of Traffic

Imagine a scene from a television or movie depiction of a classroom where students repeat back to the teacher:

> *Teacher:* Repeat after me: $2 \times 2 = 4$.
> *Class replies in unison:* $2 \times 2 = 4$
> *Teacher:* $3 \times 3 = 9$
> *Class replies in unison:* $3 \times 3 = 9$

The second "traffic lane" of working memory is the phonological loop, which is primarily involved in sound-related processing. Verbal rehearsal activates the phonological loop, and without it, memory suffers. For example, individuals with a condition called *aphasia* are unable to move their facial and mouth muscles due to brain trauma or stroke. Cognitively, they know what they want to say, but they cannot move their muscles to speak the words, which end up sounding like garbled speech. Interestingly, aphasiacs often have very poor working memory, which demonstrates the importance of verbal rehearsal for memory. In fact, as I am proofreading this paragraph, I am moving my mouth and verbally rehearsing the meaning and phrases. This verbal rehearsal helps me remember what was just written and connect it to what comes next. Perhaps you verbally recited some of the numbers in the Memory Challenge at the start of this chapter? Have you ever seen students moving their lips when they are working, silently reciting information they are trying to remember?

The phonological loop varies among individuals, with aphasiacs being an extreme example. Some students can verbalize information fluidly and commit it quickly to memory, whereas others need to work harder to build this skill. Classroom strategies to support the phonological loop of working memory include the following:

- Provide time for verbal rehearsal of new information, through such means as group discussion, peer teaching, skits, or talk-aloud.
- Integrate verbal processing strategies, such as turn and talk or "I do, we do, you do."
- Let students do more of the talking. It uncovers where they are stuck and helps them work through their understandings.

The Central Executive: The Traffic Officer

The visual sketchpad and the phonological loop are coordinated by a central executive subcomponent of working memory. The central executive is like a traffic officer directing incoming visual and phonological lanes of traffic based on information deemed necessary for a task at hand.

The central executive will coordinate the different processes, keeping focus on processing information pertinent to the goal to help build the memory. Note how important it is to have the goal clarified, so that the central executive is able to coordinate incoming information most effectively.

Novice learners may not have yet had background experiences to know how to direct attention, integrate relevant information, or process new concepts strategically. It is as though their "traffic controller" does not have the experience to know which "incoming traffic" to let through, which lanes of traffic to stop, or which cars to redirect to a different route. Learning can feel chaotic and overwhelming. By contrast, learners who are more experienced have a more experienced central executive "traffic controller" that knows how to direct the most relevant incoming information efficiently and strategically. It efficiently strategizes what information needs to be attended to, integrated, and ultimately remembered. Part of learning is becoming more strategic about how to integrate relevant incoming sensory information with preexisting understandings, much like a traffic controller who knows how to integrate traffic from many directions.

In the classroom, many strategies can be reflected upon in terms of how they support the central executive component of working memory. Here are some examples:

- Break long-term goals into clearly defined short-term goals, or "chunk" information. Doing so helps the "traffic controller" focus on a manageable amounts of information for a given period of time.

- Preview key ideas, vocabulary, and concepts before a lesson, video, or lecture. Doing so helps the "traffic controller" be on the alert for certain relevant information and let pass what is unnecessary.

- Annotate articles or readings with tips that highlight important background information.

- Provide descriptions to help analyze key information from charts, graphs, or images.

As mentioned before, all parts of working memory—the visual sketchpad, the phonological loop, and the central executive—vary among individuals. Depending on the context, students may rely more on one strategy than another, and this means working-memory deficits can look different from one class to another. In a science lab, it may seem a challenge for a learner to remember lab sequences or hold multistep cycles and processes in mind. In history class, it may manifest as a struggle to keep a train of thoughts or arguments during group discussions. Although strategies to address working memory are not new to educators, we can better understand why a technique or resource may be helpful and necessary. Understanding subcomponents of working memory can help educators intentionally design strategies into their learning environments. And don't forget that the usefulness of doing this applies not just to students. As one high school science teacher observed, "As I was walking with my colleague, I could feel the ideas we were discussing slipping away from memory. I needed to scaffold my visual sketchpad and write it down!"

Recap, Reflect, and Discuss

The model of working memory presented here describes three subcomponents of working memory: the visual sketchpad, phonological loop, and central executive. These can be used to think about how to design for learning with options for learners to visualize, verbalize, and highlight key information for memory.

With this in mind, consider the following questions for reflection and discussion:

1. Memory Challenge, Part 3: Recite the number sequence presented at the start of the chapter, but this time in reverse order. This activity relies heavily on working memory, or holding information in mind in the face of distraction.
2. How does the breakdown of the three subcomponents of working memory deepen your thinking about how to design options that scaffold memory?

Cognitive Load

So far in this chapter I have described extreme examples of memory skill and deficit and explored some subcomponents of working memory. Another way to think about memory is through the concept of *cognitive load*, or the amount of mental energy it takes to do a task. Difficult, challenging tasks or novel situations require that we expend more mental energy—they increase our cognitive load. Think of cognitive load like sand filling your brain. At the start of a lesson, students arrive with different amounts of sand. Some have very little—they have eaten well, have had adequate rest, have an activated physiology, and perceive this environment to be positive. They may have sufficient background knowledge in the content, and they have plenty of mental "space" left to take on new learning. However, other students arrive to class with lots of sand. They may be thinking about a fight with a friend or trying to comprehend the new content. Think of students who are just learning English in a math class. They are trying to hold in mind both the English language and the new math concepts. Their cognitive load "fills up" faster.

Different classroom tasks increase the metaphorical sand in the brain—or the cognitive load. Sometimes, it can feel as though we have no space left to learn anything more; we have no mental energy left. For example, my first year teaching, I was trying to tackle all of the new schedules, routines, content, students, and lesson planning. I remember getting home one night and realized that I had forgotten to get groceries for dinner. My brain was full; it was as though I had no space left to even make dinner!

Scaffolds and tools such as graphic organizers, calculators, sentence starters, annotations, or model examples can also help reduce cognitive load so learners have more mental energy to put toward the task at hand. As the demands of a task increase, including the *perceived* demands of a task and the emotional appraisals, it takes more mental effort, increases cognitive load, and can make it more challenging to get into complex levels of learning.

To support cognitive load, reflect on the requisite skills or demands in the task that students need to have in order to successfully accomplish the goal. Reduce distractions in the environment so learners do not needlessly expend cognitive energy on irrelevant tasks, and seek to have flexibility so students can minimize threats they may perceive. Here a few possibilities:

- Have flexible seating and spaces in the environment.
- Substitute irrelevant but complex vocabulary with terms that are clearer and support the intended learning. Invite students to define vocabulary they need—not just words on a list.
- Clarify subgoals as part of larger goals so each step along the way feels manageable.
- During direct instruction (e.g., read-alouds, lectures, or directions), share key information in another way, such as on chart paper, on a whiteboard, or through a PowerPoint.

Know that students are likely to appreciate your efforts. Here's what one 11th grader told his teacher: "When you gave me an outline of the information you were teaching today before class, I could spend more time listening and processing instead of just trying to keep up taking notes during the discussions. I understood more." In addition, teachers who implement strategies such as those described here come to understand the benefits. A math teacher reported, "When I thought about all the requisite skills required to do the math problem, I realized letting students use a calculator freed up their cognitive load so they could focus on the intricacies of the problem instead of simple calculations."

Memory's Location in the Brain

Where is your memory of your last birthday located in your brain? Where have you stored information about who you were with, where you went, what kind of cake you had, or your favorite gift?

Memory used to be described in terms of a "grandmother" cell theory, which proposed that there was a single brain cell for each memory. The theory suggested you would have a single brain cell that recorded the memory of your last birthday party. You may have heard news of a "Jennifer Aniston cell" or a "Halle Barry cell" that seemed to support this single-cell hypothesis of memory. The news reported a study of patients undergoing brain surgery who had single neurons fire uniquely in response to an image of the celebrity. However, this theory and related research oversimplified memory storage in the brain. If memory resided in a single cell, imagine the devastation if that one cell were damaged! Instead, we know that memories are composed of unique patterns of thousands of brain cells distributed throughout the brain that have been constructed over time.

Another, more accurate theory about the location of memory describes memory as being linked to vast networks of neurons. When you remember your grandmother, for instance, many brain networks are activated: visual networks for what she looks like, such as the texture of her hair, the shape of her face, the contours of her form, and the color of her favorite sweater. Audio networks store the sound, intonation, pitch, and rhythm of her voice. Olfactory networks store the smell of her perfume or shampoo. Throughout the brain, emotions for your grandmother activate the feelings and memories you have accumulated into a cohesive, unified understanding of her. These memories can also activate your physiology, such as heart rate and blood pressure. This theory also helps explain why sometimes a smell or sight might trigger a memory; it activates a part of a circuit involved in that memory.

Emotion, Memory, and Learning

Emotion is essential to memory. It is the knot that ties together aspects of cognition. Emotional engagement can be a tipping point for learning and can be ignited in different ways for each learner. Sometimes having a friend to work with, a little extra time, the option to draw the answer instead of write it, being able to use a particular tool for an assignment, or just knowing that the teacher likes you can make all the difference. Emotional engagement can mitigate effects of cognitive load and support the variability of learners in your classrooms.

Recap, Reflect, and Discuss

Cognitive load is the amount of energy it takes to complete a task, and it varies based on factors such as background experience and perception of resources for a task. We can offer external scaffolds to support the cognitive load inherent to tasks, so learners can focus on building higher-level skills and understandings.

Memories are not stored in just one brain cell, but are spread throughout networks, with emotion networks at the core.

With these points in mind, consider the following questions for reflection and discussion:

1. How can analyzing the cognitive load of a task help determine which resources can be used to support the learning goal? How does this connect to skill theory and the Zone of Proximal Development (ZPD) explored in Chapter 3?
2. How have you observed evidence that engagement supports memory systems?

Chapter Summary

We know there is tremendous variability in memory. Savants and individuals with memory deficits can inspire us to design strategies such as multisensory options and emotional relevancy. The three-part working memory model can inform how we design the learning environment, with options that support the visual sketchpad, the phonological loop, and the central executive. Scaffolds that reduce cognitive load enable some tasks to be offloaded so learners can focus on more complex learning challenges, or the desirable difficulties, and build interconnected, robust memory networks.

Revisiting the Educator Dilemma

We can reflect on the case of Jeff, as described at the start of the chapter, through the lens of cognitive load due to deficits in working memory. Most of the science demonstration was presented through verbal directions, so Jeff was unable to hold that information in mind—especially once the lab procedure began. This led him to look as though he had not been paying attention or that he did not care to complete the tasks. With a few additional strategies integrated into the learning environment, Jeff (and others) could focus their cognitive energy on the lab content instead of focusing on trying to remember the verbal directions. How can you make connections from this chapter to your teaching design?

Here are some ways this educator thought about supporting variability in working memory:

- **Include multisensory options,** such as drawing images that align to key steps or vocabulary, writing key steps on the board, and demonstrating the lab directions (to support the visual sketchpad). Offer options for discussion and verbal rehearsal of key parts of the lab (to support the phonological loop).

- **Offer emotional connections,** such as ways to contextualize the lab with what students already know and to real-world situations.

- **Preview and highlight key information and vocabulary** to support the central executive.

- **Reduce cognitive load** through providing copies of lecture notes related to the lab or a bulleted summary of key ideas.

As it turned out, Jeff was able and motivated to do the work; however, he struggled to hold verbal information in mind. When he had information previewed, written down, and summarized, Jeff could accomplish more of the lab's requirements independently and at a higher level.

Teacher Connection: College Lectures

Taking notes from a lecture is a complex process that relies heavily on working memory. I have changed how I design my lectures based on this understanding. First, I reflect on my goal for the lecture, which is usually to gain relevant background information on the topic of the day. Then I think about the variability of my learners; it is expected that they will vary in terms of background knowledge, vocabulary, and interest in the content. Some will have done all of the prereadings and be interested in the content; others may not have taken a course like this before or will have missed several classes and not even know what we are going to discuss. I am also aware that the expectation of listening to the lecture and recording pertinent information requires working memory skills as students must hold information in mind, organize, and record it while new information is being shared.

I use a few options to try to support working-memory demands during my lectures and to reduce cognitive load so students could focus on building higher-level content understanding. First, I highlight the critical points by writing them on the board, and then I compile and share this summary from the class discussion. I also share my PowerPoint slides with students before my lecture, and several have commented to me about how much this helps them to take notes (reducing their cognitive load). I ask students to reflect with a partner at different points during the lecture to share their own experience in relation to the topic (supporting the phonological loop). This helps me know more about what they value and find important (which helps contextualize and relates to emotion, relevancy). I have an overarching concept map of the full semester and begin class by orienting "where we are" in the scope and sequence of the broader course context (supporting the visual sketchpad). I also started to record my lectures, which I first thought would lead to fewer students attending class. I soon realized that this helped students access the information at different paces (as they can pause and rewatch parts of the video). Then my class time became more than just content delivery and maximized the opportunities for collective group collaboration around more real-world issues and meaningful experiences. With these few simple adjustments, I ended up completely transforming my class—unintentionally—and noticed more students engaged, attentive, and able to gain deeper learning during our work.

Note that when an elementary teacher heard this story from a college professor, she reflected on how it could translate to her 2nd grade classroom. During circle time, all of the information is delivered in a verbal way. She thought about how she could start to incorporate clipboards with graphic organizers for students to see information while they are discussing it.

Social Media Connections

@CogSciLearning
@TeachThought
@EquitableAccess

6 | INTRINSICALLY MOTIVATE

What we learn with pleasure, we never forget.

—Alfred Mercier

Brain Research	Design Strategies
• *Flow* is a positive state for learning. • Emotions are hard (nearly impossible) to identify in others. • "Aha" moments of insight show up as changes in brain-wave patterns.	• Provide clear goals, offer feedback on progress, and make resources available. • Build a shared language to communicate about emotions for learning. • Highlight progress, build community, and give students ownership over their learning paths (self-determination theory).

Educator Dilemma: A high school teacher expresses her puzzlement over a student named Joann, whom she describes as "generally pleasant and agreeable in class; however, she is not doing well in school." The teacher reports that Joann "is failing several classes and is not engaged in any clubs or sport teams. The most concerning part is that she does not seem motivated to improve her work, effort, or participation. She describes classes as boring, irrelevant, or too hard." Faced with this dilemma, the teacher asks, "What can I do to try to engage Joann? I do not know how to genuinely help her invest in her learning." In what ways does this educator dilemma resonate with you?

The State of Flow

Imagine a time when you were so completely absorbed in a task, time passed unnoticed. The typical distractions went undetected as you became fully immersed and absorbed in what you were doing. This condition is the state of *flow*, in which attention is focused and emotions are positively activated. It is an ideal cognitive state for learning.

Flow can happen in any context, whether reading a book, playing a sport or game, practicing an instrument, participating in a discussion, or working on an assignment or a challenging task. A few design strategies can help students achieve a state of flow during learning. First, as discussed in Chapter 1, there needs to be a clear goal. Next, the student's expectations need to align with this goal. Finally, students need timely feedback on their progress toward reaching that goal.

Flow can be maximized when there is a perception of having adequate resources for the demands of the task. Recall from Chapter 4 how important perception is for engagement and learning. Given the variability within any task, providing a few options relevant to the intended goal can empower learners to make choices that facilitate their learning and to be in a more positive state for learning. The UDL guidelines presented in Chapter 2 can help with the selection of options to optimize engagement, representation, and action and expression.

In a state of flow, there is a balance of resources and demands. If there are too many resources and the task is not very challenging, this can lead to a state of apathy or boredom. For example, if the task is to learn vocabulary words and you already know the content, having additional resources for the task will not help with engagement. By contrast, if there are inadequate resources for a challenging task, this can lead to a state of stress or anxiety. For example, if a student is working to solve a word problem but cannot decode text, does not know how to do the problem, or does not think he or she can do it, then this can lead to a state of frustration. For flow, there needs to be a balance of perceived resources and demands. "If challenges are too high, one gets frustrated, then worried, and eventually anxious. If challenges are too low relative to one's skills, one gets relaxed, then bored. If both challenges and skills are perceived to be low, one gets to feel apathetic. But when high challenges are matched with high skills, then the deep involvement that sets flow apart from ordinary life is likely to occur" (Csikszentmihalyi, 1997, p. 30).

When students understand the goal and the related expectations, and have the resources to achieve that goal, flow is more likely. If asked, the students will be able to state what they are working to achieve, and they will receive frequent feedback relevant to their progress. In a state of flow, learning is optimized (Figure 6.1). Flow can push students beyond their comfort zone and into new challenges. Note how flow also aligns with skill theory and the ZPD from Figure 3.1 (p. 68).

Looking for Engagement

How can you know if a student is engaged or in a state of flow? How do you look when you are engaged in a task? Determining student engagement can be impossible. One student may have her head

FIGURE 6.1 | Components for Achieving a State of "Flow"

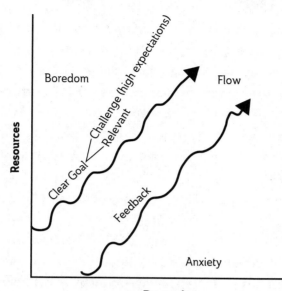

down on the desk and look disengaged but might actually be deep in thought related to the learning goal. Another student may be looking attentively at the reading but be distracted and off task completely. Engagement looks different from one individual to another and even within the same individual at different times. How can educators possibly be able to look for engagement in learning?

On a personal note, it is challenging even to recognize engagement in my own children. For example, a few summers ago we visited the Niagara Falls Cave of the Winds. As we walked under the falls, my son bundled himself tightly in his rain poncho, hunched over, and took baby steps through the walkways. I thought he was miserable, counting steps until the experience was over. By contrast, my daughter hardly donned her rain poncho, walked briskly right toward the falls, outstretched her arms, and screamed with laughter in the water. I assumed she was fully engaged in the experience. However, it turns out both kids loved the experience and described it as their favorite part of the vacation. I had entirely misinterpreted my son's emotions. For him, engagement was about leaving his comfort zone and fully perceiving the intense tactile and auditory extremes of the falls in his own quiet space. For my daughter, the engagement came from participating in the energy. The lesson here is noteworthy: even with someone we know really well, we cannot assume engagement. If I cannot even determine the engagement of my own children, how can I possibly recognize and gauge engagement of the dozens of students I see each day?

Incorporating opportunities to communicate about emotions during learning tasks is a first step to better understanding how our own affective state impacts our learning. Through building and sharing a more detailed and nuanced language for emotion and learning, we can design more effective strategies that help us better gauge students' engagement (Barrett, 2017a). Instead of ignoring or discouraging emotions for learning, as I have heard some educators do when they tell students to "check your emotions at the door," we need to instead encourage discourse about the important role of emotions for learning. We need to help learners identify and reflect on how they leveraged their emotions in service of the learning so they become more attuned to how subtle emotional signals can help them or be a barrier (Immordino-Yang & Faeth, 2010).

A mood meter, such as the RULER developed by the Yale Center on Emotional Intelligence, is a tool that can be used to support communication about emotions during learning (Nathanson, Rivers, Flynn, & Brackett, 2016). It can be used by a single student or by an entire class as a way to share appraisal and activation of emotion. Generally, the mood meter has two axes: (1) the x-axis has a positive-negative continuum, measuring "how good or bad do I feel" and (2) the y-axis has a high-low energy continuum, measuring "how energized do I feel: high or low?" Different vocabulary, fictional characters, numbers, or colors may be used to develop a more detailed language for emotion within the different quadrants of the mood meter. For example, Tigger, Elmo, the color yellow, or a +/+ value have been used to represent a state of positive, active emotion. Eeyore, the color blue, or a −/− value have been used to represent a state of negative, deactivated emotion. Oscar the Grouch, Rabbit, the color red, or a −/+ value, have been used to represent a state of negative, active emotion. And finally, Winnie the Pooh, Goofy, the color green, or a +/− value have been used to represent a state of positive, calm emotion. Each educator, class, or individual may choose a preferred way to reference and talk about the different quadrants. The important piece is that communication and self-reflection about the role of emotion during learning be more explicit.

Generally, people have a "home base" of emotion around which they fluctuate throughout the day. For example, I rate my own general home base to be a +1/+2. The various events I encounter during the day can shift me from this general starting point, and the shifts will vary from day to day or even within the same event at different times. For example, in the morning, when I have my cup of coffee and go for a jog, I tend to move to a more +/− place, but then I shift to a negative, active state (−3/+3) while driving to work in the awful Boston traffic. I would not be productive at work if I stayed in this stressed state! Essential for using the mood meter is understanding how to shift your mood to be in a place where you can do your best work for the task at hand. For example, depending on my work day, I will need different strategies to shift my emotions. If I need to present in front of colleagues, I prefer to be in a more positive, active state (+1/+3), and strategies I use to achieve this include having a few moments of quiet for myself, eating a snack, or listening to a favorite song. If I need to read and write about a journal article, which requires more of a +1/−1 range for me to do my best work, I might go into the quiet office space where there are no interruptions and do some stretching or close my eyes for a few minutes. I can use the options available in my work environment to help me shift my emotion to be in my best space for the cognitive work.

Educators can use a similar process with students to help them develop different strategies that they can leverage in order to shift their emotions to maximize learning. For example, one student may have just had a fight with a friend and starts class at a −4/+3 state. Perhaps the task (goal) in class this day is to work on a collaborative engineering project. This student may reflect that she does her best collaborative work in a more +/+ state and that she will need to use some of the options available to help her get to that state for her work. For instance, she may choose to first go to a quiet area and watch a background video that relates to the engineering project. She may decide to work independently to draft a few ideas for the project before joining her team. She may rely more on a checklist of tasks to complete. The learning still needs to be goal-driven and productive each day; however, the options learners choose from to help them be in the best emotional place for learning will vary. Note that the positive "Elmo" space is not necessarily better than other quadrants; no one wants a classroom filled with Elmos. Instead, recognize and value the variability of emotions. Use UDL or other strategies presented in this book to design a few options that may be selected by students to help each be in his or her best emotion state for learning. Share feedback not only on progress of their work but also on the strategies they chose to support their emotions for learning. Being able to recognize and have a language about how to shift your emotion to be productive is an invaluable skill that can be learned at any age and will transfer beyond the classroom.

The mood meter tool, in combination with Universal Design for Learning, is a powerful way to consciously shift design and discussion of emotions for learning. Here is a summary of how to integrate the framework:

1. **Identify your current emotion.** At the start of a learning event, reflect on your current emotion state using a mood meter. Note that there is not a "better" or a "worse" place to be on the mood meter. Variability will occur within and between learners at all times. For example, take a moment and reflect on where you would put yourself on the mood meter right now. Are you generally positive and energized, positive and relaxed, negative and energized, or negative and relaxed?

2. **Know the learning goal.** Communicate and share the goal of the task, including the purpose and expectations. For example, let's use a hypothetical scenario in which our learning goal is for you to finish reading this entire book today.

3. **Appraise where you need to be on the mood meter to do your best work.** Determine what emotion state you need to be in to do your best work toward the learning goal. For our reading example, some of you may prefer to be in more of a relaxed, "Pooh bear," +/− state. Others may prefer to be in more of a +/+ state to work toward this hypothetical goal of finishing this book today.

4. **Integrate resources available in the environment to help you achieve the learning goal.** Maximize use of the flexible options within a learning environment to help achieve the goal. This factor will be unique for each classroom or learning space, and Universal Design for Learning can be used to inform the options for how you can recruit interest, persistence, and self-regulation (Engagement); how information is presented (Representation); and how you can show your learning (Action and Expression). For our hypothetical example, your current environment likely includes options that

you can use to help yourself be in an emotionally productive state for the reading task. For example, some of you may prefer to relax, get comfortable on the couch, or get a cup of tea. Others may take short breaks in the form of brisk walks or get a partner to read aloud with and discuss the reflection questions. Again, there is no "right" or "wrong" quadrant, and what you prefer today may be different than what you will prefer tomorrow. The important part is to do what you need to achieve the goal.

5. **Reflect on the progress.** During work, pause to reflect on specific progress that was made toward the intended learning goal. How did different strategies support or not support your effort? Ultimately, learners become better at self-regulating and selecting appropriate resources to maximize high-level learning. They may become better at recognizing when a particular strategy is not working and shift. For example, you may determine that you are feeling tired and not understanding what you are reading, so you may need to switch to a new strategy, such as taking notes in the margins or on sticky notes. You may determine that you are not challenged enough and want to jump ahead to the book's summary questions to check whether you need to read that section. In many ways, the role of educators is to help facilitate the learning environment to maximize emotional and cognitive learning (Van Geert & Steenbeek, 2008).

Using a mood meter aligns to core features of flow because both focus on having a goal, resources, and process-based feedback (see Figure 6.2). In addition, the mood meter helps us to recognize how our affective state influences our learning.

Mood meters can be used to amass class data. For example, an educator may ask students to place an anonymous sticker on the

FIGURE 6.2 | Sample Mood Meter

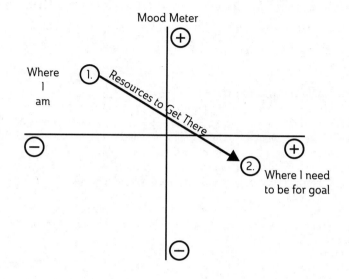

mood meter as they enter the room. Based on the general mood of the class, the teacher may incorporate a class activity to help shift the general class affect. For example, if an entire class reports being in a more tired, deactivated state and the activity is to have a vigorous debate, then the teacher may do a quick energizing activity with the entire class. Although individual emotional states will vary, some strategies have a tendency to generally "move" a class or an individual to a different state. Here are some examples:

- To encourage a positive, active state, use humor, movement, discussions, collaboration, or stations. Perhaps have the lights bright and play upbeat music.

- To encourage a positive, less active state, use readings, puzzle problems, or journaling. You may close the curtains or lower the lights.

- To encourage a negative, active state, use challenging brain teasers, a controversial image, or a statement to rouse discussion.

- To encourage a negative, less active state, tell a poignant story, have a moment of silence with a reflection prompt, or share appropriate imagery.

Recap, Reflect, and Discuss

Emotions are central to learning, yet it is nearly impossible to determine another's emotions. Therefore, we need to better recognize and communicate about emotions during learning. We can incorporate the three components required for flow (clear goals, resources, and feedback) or use a mood meter to share emotion states and leverage resources that are aligned with UDL to help self-regulate for the intended goal.

With these points in mind, consider the following questions for reflection and discussion.

1. When do you remember being in a state of flow? What was the goal and how were your resources and demands balanced?
2. In what ways could you use a mood meter tool to reflect with learners on how different resources help each shift emotions for productive learning?

Intrinsic Motivation and Self-Determination Theory

The Tour de France is an international bicycle race through the steep Pyrenees and Alps mountains. It spans 21 segments over 23 days, and the 2,200-mile course includes some of the world's most sheer slopes to challenge the cyclists. One of the challenging ascents is Mont Ventoux, a 10-mile climb at a 9 percent gradient at the end of one of the race days. The riders persist through torrential rainfall and extreme heat, through crazed fans and painful falls, through hunger and muscle cramping. What helps drive motivation for cyclists to persist through such conditions each day?

Similarly, a student decides to stay after class to ask deeper questions about a topic, spends hours seeking additional information to learn more, and creates an elaborate project that exceeds expectations. What leads to such intrinsic motivation? How can the design of learning environments support motivation and ignite curiosity to want to learn beyond the requirements?

Self-determination theory (SDT) is "an empirically supported and comprehensive model of human motivation" (Deci & Ryan, 2008, p. 182). It describes how curiosity drives individuals to learn and explains that motivation comes from wanting to satisfy a curiosity. Self-determination theory has three key core components: (1) competency, (2) relatedness, and (3) autonomy. Let's examine each in turn and consider how we can design these components in our learning environments.

Competency

Competency refers to the perception of effectiveness—that you are making progress. Small victories can go a long way in terms of emotional engagement and learning. Along the entire Tour de France, there are progress signs with messages such as "2 km left" or "You have passed 4 of the 7 climbs for today." Fans line the entire course, yelling, "You can do it," "The top of the climb is within sight," and other words of encouragement. These external factors support a feeling of competency and internal belief that you are capable of making progress toward the challenges at hand. They can translate to self-talk about competency that can motivate during challenging times, such as "I trained with hills just like this; I know what to do when my legs have a burning cramp."

Educators can explicitly design learning events for competency. Here are some examples, as already shared in this book but that also connect with designing for competency:

- Offer specific, process-based feedback about the progress that is being made toward the high-level goal; for example, "Your outline contains three of the key details; you need two more";

or "The steps you used in the math problem are correct; see if you can find the addition mistake."

- Chunk a long-term project or goal into smaller, manageable parts, so progress is visible. "Today we will complete the research table, tomorrow we will incorporate the content into the essay structure, and then we will put them together with transition sentences." A higher education professor had weekly assignments build to a final research paper, and the students remarked about how proud they were of the final outcome and how the process seemed so manageable. The professor noted how much better the quality of the work became with the addition of the weekly steps.

- Share your confidence that each student can achieve the high expectation; for example, "This is a challenging task, but you have helpful resources to use, and I have confidence you can do it."

- Have students self-report on their progress and strategies that helped them achieve a goal; for example, a student shared the following on an exit ticket: "I used the acronym to help me remember the steps for solving the equation."

Relatedness

Riders in the Tour de France are part of a team. About nine riders work throughout the race to ensure each has adequate water, food, and resources. Sometimes one member of the team will make an extra effort to ensure the success of another teammate. In the 2016 Tour de France, for example, the leading rider from one team fell on a slippery descent in the rain, and instantly another teammate offered the leader his bike so that he could continue his progress. The team had a common goal: they were working together to achieve, and success depended on the contributions of each member.

This aspect of the Tour de France relates to the second component of self-determination theory: *relatedness*, or the interaction and connection among individuals. In a classroom, relatedness is a part of the overall culture and climate that takes time and routines to build. Such a culture includes conversations about different ways with which learners can contribute to the community. Variability is valued. The actions and attitudes of each person matter; if a single student is negative, it can have subtle ripple effects on the rest of the class. We are not isolated brains; we are always immersed in and interacting within our environment, classrooms, school, and communities. How we relate to and understand one another is important for establishing safe spaces learning.

Empathy is the ability to experience the feelings of others and put yourself in their shoes, and it is a critical element of relatedness. Neurologically, empathy activates deep systems in our brain, such as the anterior insula (which monitors the feelings of your gut) and the midbrain (which monitors your blood pressure and breath rate). Empathy activates your medulla, the very part of your brain that keeps your heart beating. This is powerful to understand. When we attune to others' experiences, it activates the very systems of our brain that help keep us alive! How we foster collaboration and community affects the physiology of each learner.

Flexible work options empower learners to have the agency to make choices they need. Some strategies that support relatedness include the following:

- Interact with students as they enter and leave the classroom. Let them know that you value them as individuals and support them in their learning.

- Foster collaboration through modeling and by being clear about expectations for group work so each learner knows what he or she is working on and how each contribution matters to the success of the team.

- Offer opportunities for students to give one another feedback, so it is not just the teacher who holds the feedback. Having clear rubrics with subjective language clarified (e.g., define *strong effort* or *good team player* by explicitly sharing what each looks like and how can it be objectively assessed).

- Allow students to laugh and to be silly. Learning is hard work and takes energy. A little laughter may reduce some cognitive load, enhance the perception of the context, and help build community.

- Have mutually agreed-upon social and group norms so learners are part of the agreement. This works for learners of all ages, including those in higher education.

- Model and share your learning challenges and strategies so students see you as an active learner in the community; for example, "When I had trouble understanding X, I tried Y. What do you think you might do?"

- Celebrate diversity in ways that value the uniqueness of your learners.

Autonomy

In the Tour de France, each cyclist is an expert rider; however, each trained for the event in a different way. Although there are some common essential training elements to build toward expertise, such as strength, endurance, and flexibility, each racer integrated these elements differently into a preparation routine that worked best for himself. The racers had options for how they approached their training, worked with the team, set up their daily routines, and built their competence.

Autonomy, the third component of self-determination theory, recognizes the importance of independence and choice as elements that support motivation (see Chapter 4). Being able to choose how or when to use a strategy, to take risk, or to take a break is empowering. It is also important for learners to take ownership for the decisions and consequences of their choices; this is a core component of learning. During the course of the school day, learners often have little autonomy over their learning. Assuming some element of control over the learning process builds stronger intrinsic motivation and can make it more likely learners will want to go beyond requirements. Design strategies that support autonomy include the following:

- Present clear expectations and share options (even if only one or two!) for learners to set their own learning path.

- Use the UDL guidelines to integrate options for engagement, representation, and action and expression for the learning target. Note how the UDL guidelines have the stated goal of building "expert learners" who are purposeful and motivated, resourceful and knowledgeable, and strategic and goal-directed. What do these look like in your discipline or for students in your context?

- Reflect with students about which choices optimized their progress and learning and which were barriers.

"Aha!" Moments of Insight

One of the most satisfying moments for an educator is when a learner experiences an "Aha!" moment, or an insight around an important concept, a way to solve a problem, or a new perspective. Such a moment can seem to appear as if by magic and yields a deeper level of understanding or seeing a problem in a new way that, once seen, cannot be unseen.

A classic example that illustrates an "aha" moment involves what is called the Necker cube illusion (Figure 6.3). At first glance, the image is simply a three-dimensional cube. However, this ambiguous

FIGURE 6.3 | **Necker Cube**

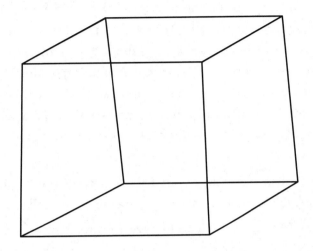

figure can be perceived in two ways. Focusing on the left side of the cube brings the left square to the front, whereas focusing on one of the other corners of the cube shifts the orientation so that the cube now appears to point upward, to the right. Take a moment to play with your perception of this switch and experience an "aha" moment when both perspectives are apparent.

Neurologically, changes in the brain during an "aha" moment have been studied with electroencephalograms (EEGs). Electroencephalograms use electrodes on the surface of the scalp to detect changes in electrical activity of the brain over time, which are documented as five main kinds of oscillations (Figure 6.4). *Alpha waves* occur in quiet, but awake, relaxed states. *Beta waves* are prevalent during the most active, attentive, decision-making moments. *Gamma waves*, the highest-frequency waves, are active during intense focus, when background distractions are suppressed; these are of special interest as they seem to play a significant role in unifying multiple brain networks that may help create a conscious experience. *Theta waves* are observed in states of relaxed meditation or drowsiness, and *delta waves* are involved in non-REM or deep sleep.

FIGURE 6.4 | Brain Waves as They Appear on an Electroencephalogram

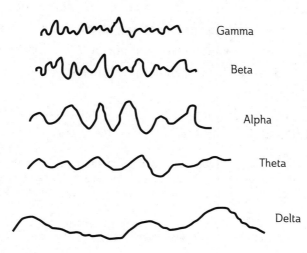

About one second before we experience an "aha" moment, or the moment where we gain new insights or clarity around a problem, there is an increase in alpha-wave activity. It is as though we are tuning out the world around us for a moment. Then there is a spike of gamma-wave activity, where multiple brain-network activities are being unified. For example, evidence indicates that there is actually simultaneous recruitment of the "looking-out" and default mode (DM) networks. Recall from Chapter 3 that these networks tend to work in opposition to each other, but before an "aha" moment, they seem to cooperate in a unique way.

How might we design for these incredibly rewarding "aha" moments of insight? Evidence shows that being in a slightly more positive state, such as the +/+ quadrant of a mood meter, is ideal. In addition, there is evidence that having time and space for quiet reflection during the day is important. Because learners will vary in how and when they achieve quiet, positive activation, it is important for lesson design and classroom spaces to include flexibility for this.

Activate thought-provoking questions to incite reflection and integrate multiple networks. Reframe complex information, problems, or processes from different perspectives, and encourage both active, collaborative work as well as quieter options to allow the mind to wander and close out the external environment.

Recap, Reflect, and Discuss

Competence, relatedness, and autonomy are three core features of self-determination theory (SDT) that support intrinsic engagement for learning. "Aha" moments of insight require an opportunity for quiet reflective time and a convergence of brain activity.

With this in mind, consider the following questions for reflection and discussion:

1. Reflect on strategies you already use to support each part of SDT: competency, relatedness, and autonomy.
2. What challenges do you face in building relatedness, including the climate and culture in your learning environment?
3. How do you work to build empathy and encourage different perspectives with your learners?

Chapter Summary

Learning environments can be purposefully designed to support intrinsic motivation using insights from the theory of flow, self-determination theory, and tools such as the mood meter. A state of flow—when you are fully engrossed in a task—is a positive state for learning. Factors that support flow include having a clear goal, process-based feedback toward that goal, and relevant resources for meeting the demands of a task. Building a context that supports competency, relatedness, and autonomy (the three components of self-determination theory) also encourages intrinsic motivation. Noticing successes, making progress, and feeling like a contributing member of the community support competency and relatedness.

Allowing students some autonomy in how they use flexible options can also support intrinsic motivation.

We know that emotion is essential for learning. However, it is challenging for educators to know if learners are engaged in a task just by looking at them. The mood meter, in conjunction with UDL, provides a way to build communication and language about emotions and learning. First, evaluate your current appraisal and activation (where you are now), then determine where you need to go (the learning goal). Then integrate strategies that will help you attain a positive state for you to move toward the targeted learning goals. What works well for one may not work for another, and the same strategy may not work for the same learner at every time. Variability is guaranteed. When we design for both active and reflective learning, more learners may encounter those amazing "aha" moments in their learning.

Revisiting the Educator Dilemma

Let's return to the educator dilemma at the start of the chapter, which described Joann, who seems unengaged in classwork and other school activities. How can you make connections from this chapter to your teaching? Several design strategies may be integrated into her learning environment to inspire intrinsic motivation:

- **Share thoughts about the role of emotions during learning.**
  Encourage learners to use a mood meter to communicate
  how positive/negative and activated/deactivated they feel.
  Joann noticed she was less engaged when she had to read.
  Recognizing this barrier helped her talk with her teacher
  about when she could use text-to-speech options or read with
  a friend. Sometimes, of course, she would need to read on her
  own and needed to learn the strategies that helped her with
  that, but other times the reading method could be flexible.

- **Support competency.** For example, use a checklist for students to monitor progress during a work period and celebrate small steps. When Joann saw the few tasks she needed to do, it felt less overwhelming. The teacher noticed she accomplished a little more each day, even if only one item.
- **Support relatedness.** Develop agreed-upon norms for collaboration so that each team member contributes in a safe and supportive way and knows how to hold one another (and themselves) accountable.
- **Encourage autonomy.** Offer flexible pathways and strategies students can use to achieve a goal.
- **Offer opportunity for quiet reflection and active collaboration to encourage "aha" moments.** Joann actually liked to put on her headphones during independent work time, and this helped her to be less distracted. The teacher had several playlists that students could choose from.

Joann's teacher noted that introducing the mood meter allowed more targeted conversations with Joann about the learning goals and her choices related to those goals. Together, they began to notice when Joann became more disengaged and then problem-solved other options that Joann could use to engage in the work. This took a while and was not a perfect process, but it began a more open dialogue.

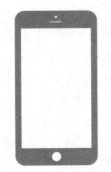

Social Media Connections

#SelfDeterminationTheory
@Brain_Facts_org
@FindingFlow

SUPPORT
THE EMOTION
OF TEACHING

I've learned that people will forget what you said, people will forget what you did, but people will never forget how you made them feel.

—Maya Angelou

Educator Dilemma: Ms. Reilly has been teaching for over 20 years and generally enjoys her job. She likes getting to know each of her students and works hard to try to connect with each one. She has a well-refined repertoire of curricular and classroom strategies that took her years to build, and they generally work well. Lately, however, she has been feeling more overwhelmed. She feels external pressures to ensure that students perform well on standardized tests and to integrate new district initiatives. These priorities don't often seem like they are supporting deep, meaningful learning in her class. She also doesn't feel she has adequate time or resources to make effective changes to her lessons. For the first time in her career, she has counted the number of days until summer vacation. How might she reengage her own passion for teaching? In what ways does this educator dilemma resonate with you?

Fast and Slow Circuits of Emotion

If a fox wanders into your backyard, this frightening stimulus can instantly activate a cascade of physiological events (see Chapter 1). Your previous experiences and expectations related to a fox are activated, alerting your attention (see Chapter 4) to important cues in the environment, such as an escape route. Your sympathetic (stress) nervous system increases your heart rate, breath rate, and glucose release to muscles; and chemicals, such as adrenaline and cortisol, flood your body so you can immediately respond with action. Perhaps you run away or try to scare the fox by making loud noises. Either way, there is no time to deliberate. Neurologically, this fast circuit of emotion immediately activates your brain and body physiology to respond to the threat in your environment. It does not wait for slower cortical interpretations or additional sensory information—it makes fast judgments and takes action.

However, input from higher-order cortical networks can offer important insights into the situation. For example, the verntromedial prefrontal cortex (vmPFC) acts like an intermediary connecting the feeling of the body during the emotional moment with the choices and actions you take. It helps you contextualize this situation and remember from past experiences: the "fox" is actually your neighbor's dog that has gotten out of the yard. There is no need to flee the scene, but the more appropriate response is to call your neighbor. Such higher-order cortical networks "rein in" the fast-acting initial appraisals, help your system return to a homeostatic balance, and help you process the context and take appropriate actions in the situation.

Note that damage to the vmPFC can also impair your ability to learn from your mistakes (Bechara et al., 2005).

Any stressor or stimulus from the environment—such as a fox in your yard, an unruly student, or a teacher evaluation—can trigger emotion networks to activate your physiology. Your past experiences and expectations influence perception and direct attention and action. Sometimes, you may make a rash decision or fall into negative behavior patterns only to later reflect on the feeling of your body in that emotional moment within the context, including the choices and actions that were taken. In the fast-paced, stimulus-filled daily routines of the classroom, relatively benign behaviors or stressors can seem much greater. We do not always have time to pause and reflect on the best course of action as we are in more of a response mode.

In addition to external stimuli, stressors can originate from within the mind, such as being nervous about an upcoming lesson or anticipating a difficult parent-teacher conference. If there is consistent stress in an environment or continued worry or dread, these physiological systems remain in a heightened state and may not return to a homeostatic balance. This can have long-term negative effects on the body and can lead to cognitive changes such as less flexibility or patience, impaired memory, or disruption in motivation and creative problem solving. This can be exemplified by a 4th grade teacher's reflection: "I just had no patience left, so the smallest behavior would aggravate me." Just as emotion is at the core of learning for students, it is also at the core of a teacher's experience in the classroom.

Emotional Energy

Teaching is emotional work—which it must be if it is to be effective. If teaching were just about delivering content, any person or any digital device could do it; we could be decontextualized from the experience. In fact, a computer program could deliver the information for mass consumption. However, learning is not linear or sequential; it is dynamic, complex, and variable. It requires active interaction between the individual and the learning environment—and there must be emotion to drive engagement for learning.

In the introduction to this book, I described the chain of events that unfolded for me on the night of my emotional "Super Bowl meltdown." I was a science teacher, teaching logical, objective content such as the scientific method and the stages of cell division. However, I was also experiencing and reacting to the learning journeys of each of my students, which was predominately emotional. I was aware of their attention and their slightest frustrations, and I relished their successes. I was their daily cheerleader, encouraging their progress, and I thought about their challenges every day. This investment of emotional energy was worth it; it created a positive, respectful learning environment that celebrated variability. However, I was exhausted at the end of every school day, and so the thought of not having a day off after the Super Bowl pushed me into my meltdown.

Approximately 20 percent of teachers do not return after just a few years in the classroom. Reasons range from a lack of support, conditions in the environment, or feeling they have inadequate time and resources to successfully teach. The demands on teachers are plentiful, from following administrative procedures, communicating with parents, integrating use of new technologies, teaching a full schedule of classes, creating lesson plans, knowing the details of the curriculum scope and sequence, and following through with classroom management strategies. In addition, teaching involves a plethora of intangible emotional components. As one teacher put it, "You feel personally responsible for every single failure or success of your students; you even dream about them! I was well prepared for the logistics and

routines of teaching, but not the emotional demands of this job."
A high school English teacher experienced serious consequences
of the emotional context of teaching: "Midway through the school
year I was taken to the emergency room. They did all sorts of tests;
however, there was nothing physiologically wrong with me. I was
just exhausted."

How can teachers achieve and maintain the high level of emotional energy required to sustain effective teaching practices? To
begin with, an important consideration is that we need to recognize that teachers are variable. Each will have unique background
experiences, expectations, and feelings of competence, relatedness,
and desire for autonomy. One teacher may get fully engaged and
recharged through preparation and design of lesson plans in a sol-
itary environment, whereas another may thrive through conversations and interactions with students or colleagues. One may energize
by engaging in independent online coursework to deepen content
expertise, whereas another prefers collaboration or a face-to-face
training session to learn about a current topic in education. It is
important for educators to discover and be able to advocate for strategies that help them not only deepen their content expertise but also
rebuild the emotional energy needed throughout the school day and
school year. Doing so is essential for effective teaching.

The design of school environments can support educators' variability and engagement. This design can be purposeful and goal
driven, and aim to mitigate the emotional exhaustion common to
teaching and help teachers experience moments of flow in the
course of their work. The strategies outlined in the next sections
align with the topics and suggestions presented so far in this book,
but this time the strategies are approached with the purpose of
supporting *teachers'* emotional engagement. Although there is no
one strategy that can work for every educator, the ideas presented

here can be used as a starting place for reflection, conversation, or change in your context.

Activate Learning (Chapter 1)

A teacher's daily schedule is generally a set schedule of courses, planning, and advising that is filled to capacity and includes commitments beyond the school day, such as chaperoning events, hosting parent meetings, coaching sports, or sponsoring after-school clubs. Teachers rarely relax—even for lunch, as that time is valued as an opportunity to plan their lessons or to offer extra help to students. They share a host of other nonteaching responsibilities during the school day, such as hall monitoring, lunch duty, and the setup and cleanup of classroom labs, lessons, and activities.

Each of these events will activate a teacher's physiology in a unique way. Some will not have enough activation and may feel bored or apathetic about the demands of the day, whereas others will have too much activation and feel stress or anxiety. Because of this variability, having flexible options in the design of the school context for managing these daily routines and responsibilities can help keep each teacher's physiology in a positively active state.

Make goals for the different tasks educators need to accomplish salient, and when possible, offer flexible, relevant options to achieve the goals. When teachers know the goals, they can choose which options they prefer. Perhaps a goal is to improve student supervision during lunchtime. One teacher may volunteer for lunch duty, enjoying the conversation and energy of the students. Another teacher may prefer to offer and supervise a quieter venue, such as a lunch nook that includes board games and reading materials. Both are actively participating in the school community and working to support the goal, but they have flexibility in how they are able to execute the goal.

Design for Variability (Chapter 2)

The Universal Design for Learning framework can be used to think about the predictable variability among educators in terms of their engagement, recognition, and strategic networks. Given this variability, proactive planning can optimize the options that are available. Here are some suggestions for such planning:

- **Offer UDL options for engagement.** At the core of UDL is a focus on engagement. Recall that UDL defines engagement in terms of recruiting interest, sustaining effort and persistence, and self-regulation. Consider how educators have opportunities to collaborate. For example, reconfigure workspaces with flexible options such as dim lighting, headphones, and comfortable chairs for quiet, independent work; a treadmill or a collaborative table in the faculty room. Ensure that any demands placed on educators, such as integration of new standards, programs, or technologies, include adequate resources, opportunities for learning, and time to support the work. One administrator offered this illustrative reflection: "I knew I had put new demands on my teachers this year, including a new reading curriculum. But I did not stop to think about how I might offer resources to support their work." It is important for educators to be able to self-reflect on their effectiveness and to recognize areas they want to iterate and improve upon.

- **Offer UDL options for representation.** Offer information to teachers beyond stand-and-deliver faculty meetings, and provide opportunities for them to deepen their professional knowledge and background. Throughout the year, reflect on flexible ways that information can be shared, such as virtual faculty meetings, e-mail news updates, or group discussions. Make information accessible digitally, verbally, through video, or using images or graphs. Incorporate opportunities for key background information from meetings or workshops to be summarized and highlighted. Have different opportunities for professional learning.

- **Offer UDL options for action and expression.** Reflect on how teachers are able to demonstrate expertise and share their work, progress, or successful teaching strategies. Provide time for verbal or digital feedback for school-related events, policies, or decisions. Share model examples, checklists, and templates for administrative tasks, such as grading procedures, website development, or parent-student communication. Encourage flexible ways to communicate about what is happening in the classroom with the community, such as using social media or highlighting teacher work in newsletters. One administrator integrated a monthly poll on an issue related to the school community and found that the quick feedback from teachers was informative, helped the teachers feel they were part of the decision-making process, and eliminated the need for additional face-to-face meetings.

Foster the Development of Brain Networks (Chapter 3)

We foster the development of brain networks through our interactions with the environment. Although an educator may demonstrate some teaching techniques and behaviors with relative ease, we can always identify areas that are challenging or could be strengthened or deepened. Hard work and effort can make a difference. Provide progress-based feedback to educators, not just evaluative summaries, and take time to ask what their pedagogical goals are for a lesson, a semester, or the year (so your feedback can be relevant and directed). Ask how they are working to achieve those goals and what tools or systems might best support their work. Share a resource bank of ideas educators can use to design for student engagement and learning. The brain has incredible plasticity, and its networks will sculpt and change based on the interactions teachers have with the learning environments. Schools should be places of learning for educators, too.

Captivate Attention (Chapter 4)

Educators have a rich array of background experiences, cultural histories, and interests. They pay attention and glean meaning from each situation in a unique way. Routines within the scope of the day and year can help educators focus on the necessary procedures and protocols. However, injecting some novelty within the year, to "shake up" the routine, can also enhance engagement. For example, there may be a great video of an exemplary teacher practice or a new "out-of-the-ordinary" resource to explore each month. Offer a "BYOI" (Bring Your Own Idea) faculty meeting to share favorite tools or resources. How might music, a guest presenter, or food liven up a faculty meeting? Provide autonomy for educators to make their own choices for resources they use and how they contribute to the community and deepen their own learning in a way that is meaningful to them.

Support Memory (Chapter 5)

Feelings of exhaustion or being burned out will come at different points during an academic year for each educator. When cognitive load is at maximum capacity, demands will seem to outweigh any resources that may be available, and this imbalance can lead to less cognitive flexibility, creativity, or working memory. Strategies that support cognitive load can mitigate these professional hazards, such as having options available for professional learning teams (such as

PLCs), peer mentoring, or coaching. Look to reduce responsibilities that pull an educator from the core teaching and student responsibilities that need to remain the focus. Educators always benefit from having additional work time, so perhaps shorten a meeting or shift the schedule to allow for an additional work period once a week. A little flexibility in this area can go a long way for teacher engagement and maintenance of emotional energy. Find opportunities to laugh together and celebrate successes throughout the year.

Intrinsically Motivate (Chapter 6)

Becoming absorbed in moments during the workday, or being in a state of flow, can build and sustain teacher engagement. It can increase motivation and persistence to put forth the effort and energy necessary for effective and engaging teaching. Use the three components of self-determination theory to build opportunities to demonstrate and feel competency. Find ways to build relatedness among the staff during work hours (rather than adding to evening demands), such as using ice breakers or teaming activities. Consider ways to communicate or self-reflect about emotions. How might educators use a mood meter to think about their current emotional state, where they need to shift in order to do their best teaching, and how to gain resources, time, or strategies to be effective?

We know that teaching is emotional work, and it is the emotion that is essential for learning to take place. One teacher summed up the situation this way: "We have such a passionate profession—emotions affect us all the time. It's the best and worst part of our job." Given the pace and rigidity of school-day schedules, look for flexibility and ways to engage and value educators. With options that support emotion and engagement, educators will be prepared not only to teach more effectively but also to continue to grow and learn themselves.

Understanding My Super Bowl Meltdown

In hindsight, I can see that I did not do a good job of self-regulating my own emotional energy during the school year that led to my Super Bowl meltdown. I now reflect with a fresh perspective on strategies I could have proactively integrated into my daily routines that may have mitigated my feelings of being overwhelmed with exhaustion. My physiology was in the "stress" state, and I felt the demands outweighed the available resources. Recognizing this would have been a first step to being able to proactively change some of my day-to-day strategies and actions. The Super Bowl took place in the middle of our cold New England winter, and the short days and the icy, early-morning, lengthy commute weighed on me. Exercise is one way that I destress, and I had not made time for that. The daily routines and structures were in place; however, I could have benefitted from integrating some aspect of novelty—perhaps to learn something new, have coffee with a colleague, take a walk during the day, or shake up the routine a bit. Feeling more autonomy in terms of my time and reflecting on my own emotional state would have benefitted me and may have averted the collapse.

Many of the ideas shared in this chapter are likely ones you already use in your routines; however, my hope is that the brain science related to variability, brain plasticity, and the central role of emotion for learning will deepen your understanding of why those strategies work.

Recap, Reflect, and Discuss

It is important to integrate flexible options that support educator variability, to have clear goals, and to use strategies as described in the chapters of this book to think about how the design of the school community can support engagement for teaching.

With this in mind, consider the following questions for reflection and discussion:

1. What professional goals do you have for yourself this year?
2. What are some options you can incorporate into the environment that support the goals, demands, and challenges of your routines?

Chapter Summary

Effective teaching is emotional work, which may partly explain the high rate of teacher burnout and attrition. It is therefore essential that we design strategies to support teachers' emotions and engagement for their own learning and practice. We need to build a more explicit language and vocabulary related to emotions for learning and teaching. Doing so ultimately supports student learning.

Strategies to support educator engagement include activating learning; valuing and designing for variability using UDL options for engagement, representation, and action and expression; fostering the development of brain networks through feedback and reflection; captivating attention using routines and novelty; scaffolding memory systems to reduce cognitive load; and intrinsically motivating through competency, relatedness, and autonomy. Educators can incorporate these strategies for themselves, or they can work with small teams or professional learning groups to build and implement strategies that are useful and that may be shared at a systems level. Ultimately, the goal is to deepen awareness and discussion about how emotion is essential for learning and how we can design for it. Get into a state of flow at work, where you are so engaged in the moment that time seems to hold still. Share the emotions you are experiencing and which strategies help you do your best work. Embolden a passion for the incredible emotional work of teaching.

Revisiting the Educator Dilemma

Recall the anecdote at the start of this chapter about Ms. Reilly, a veteran teacher who, for the first time in her career, wondered how she could recharge her passion for learning. Here's what happened to help address her dilemma. How can you make connections from this chapter to your professional context?

Instead of a prescribed professional development series for teachers, the school started to allow teachers to define their own professional learning goals and to have flexible options to accomplish that learning, either through online offerings or a face-to-face workshop series. As a veteran teacher, Ms. Reilly felt comfortable with her classroom-management skills, so she decided to focus on learning more about her content area of expertise, as history was her passion. She chose an online-course option that was offered through the district, and she was really looking forward to having this time to pursue something that was relevant for her, not just the standard, "one-size-fits-all" professional development training she typically had to attend. Ms. Reilly's reenergizing experience incorporated the following strategies:

- **Activate learning.** There were clear goals and flexible options enabling Ms. Reilly to learn. During the opening faculty meeting, she clarified the overarching goals she had for the school year with her supervisor, and they brainstormed options that would help her achieve those goals, such as finding dedicated time in the schedule for her to learn.

- **Design for variability.** All educators from the school district had options for their professional learning in terms of how they wanted to build new background knowledge (option for representation), how they would share their learning with the staff at the end of the year (option for action and expression), and how they would receive feedback and engage in collaboration during the year (options for engagement).

- **Foster the development of brain networks.** Ms. Reilly recognized through her interactions with the learning environment that she was building her brain. Although at her age she was fairly set in her ways, she knew she could build new patterns with work, effort, and feedback. She had opportunities throughout the year for reflection and progress monitoring.

- **Captivate attention.** Ms. Reilly worked to create routines that were predictable for her online professional development work, and she also had a few opportunities during the year to "change it up" with other teachers to hear about their learning.

- **Scaffold memory.** The school year could get really busy, and Ms. Reilly tried to proactively plan her online work for times she knew she would have the cognitive capacity to focus and engage. She used a visual portfolio to document her learning. She knew strategies that helped her when her brain felt "full."

- **Intrinsically motivate.** Ms. Reilly identified a few other teachers who shared a passion for history and found time to network with them (relatedness). Checking off items on her list helped her feel a sense of progress (competency). She used a mood meter and noted which strategies best helped her learning, especially when she was not feeling motivated. She used the language in the UDL guidelines to communicate more clearly about learning with her colleagues and students.

Social Media Connections

@EdWeekTeacher
#CoTeachat
@edutopia
#observeme

CONCLUSION: EMOTION TIES THE KNOT FOR LEARNING

The real voyage of discovery consists not in seeking new landscapes but in having new eyes.

—Marcel Proust

I truly believe everyone can learn. As I have emphasized in the preceding chapters, at the core of learning is emotion; emotion ties the knot for learning. Emotions are constructed from our experiences. They activate our physiology and influence what we perceive, how we pay attention, how we are motivated to act, and what we remember. Individuals vary in terms of what engages them and which strategies help them achieve learning goals. We can design learning environments that support this variability so all learners can achieve high-level learning outcomes.

157

A colleague once noted that students fail by design. Throughout this book, I have argued that the design of learning experiences (including classroom environments and curricular goals, assessments, methods, and materials) can activate physiology and direct attention, memory, and motivation. It can engage us; the design of the context matters. It is our responsibility to create environments that support engagement for learning. When we put engagement first, learning will follow. Ultimately, learners will become more self-reflective about what helps them do their best work and how to leverage emotions and resources to achieve the goals. Even on "bad days," strategies can be integrated to engage in meaningful and productive work. Students who face some of the most extreme challenges, such as homelessness, hunger, and social-emotional hardships, will have opportunities to progress toward learning goals integrating design strategies that support emotions for learning. These are lifelong-learning skills that extend beyond the walls of the classroom.

Concepts from this book can be applied both for students in learning contexts and for educators in their professional contexts. Workplace environments designed for the variability of emotions support progress toward high-level, goal-driven professional learning. Each individual is empowered to choose his or her own path for work, and the essential first step to get started is to have a clear goal and flexible, relevant options to activate emotions.

When we reflect on responses from students about how they feel about school, most center on a lack of engagement: "School is boring"; "I just do what I have to do to get by"; "I spend a lot of time looking out the window"; "I try to get out of class as often as possible." When we ask educators about challenges they face in teaching, most responses center on engagement: "I want to improve student engagement," "I want to motivate my students." Unintended consequences that may ensue if we do not design for emotion can be dire: apathy, stress, behavior disruptions, dropping out.

Throughout this book, we have explored how brain science can inform emotional design for learning. Evident from brain science is that (1) emotions are essential for learning, (2) there is tremendous variability between individuals, (3) the brain can change (plasticity) throughout life, and (4) experience and background matter. The activation model shows that too little or too much activation can prevent attention and motivation. Thinking about learner variability supplants the use of labels that can pigeonhole both student and teacher expectations. With a clear goal, flexible options informed by the UDL guidelines, and process-based feedback, we are more likely to tie the knot for a lifetime of learning through engagement.

Learning is a complex interaction between the individual and the environment (nurture), and our brain networks can be sculpted; even the expression of genes (nature) can change from what we do. Our experiences and expectations drive our attention, and emotions are at the center of what we perceive from the environment. When we perceive the context to be negative, that is the reality we will construct. When we perceive there to be some choices, opportunities, and high expectations, we can integrate the flexible options from the intentionally designed environment to achieve the goals. Routines and novelty can be balanced, and we can use understanding of concepts such as the visual sketchpad, the phonological loop, and the central executive to scaffold working memory and reduce cognitive load. We can pay attention to how we support competence, relatedness, and autonomy for intrinsic motivation in our classrooms.

We cannot assume to know whether a student is engaged; we need to build a common language to better understand how our emotions are influencing our behaviors, actions, and learning. This will allow us to better communicate and be more purposeful in the strategies we integrate to engage learners. Perhaps through these ideas, we can foster a love for learning that grows the next generation of emotionally engaged, self-directed, empathetic citizens who are lifelong learners.

Reflect and Discuss

1. How have your views of the role of emotion for engagement and learning shifted as you read this book?

2. What strategies do you already use that align to concepts discussed in this book? How can you reflect on those strategies through the new lens of emotions to engage the brain?

3. What new strategies or ideas will you integrate into the design of your learning environment? What will you share with your learners? In what ways can you start to build a more robust language that supports emotion for learning?

APPENDIX: ADDITIONAL INFORMATION ABOUT THE UDL FRAMEWORK

[T]he external environment must provide options that can equalize accessibility by supporting learners who differ in initial motivation, [and] self-regulation skills.

—National Center on Universal Design for Learning

Universal Design for Learning (UDL) was inspired in part by the architectural framework known as Universal Design (UD), which promotes the design of architectural structures that are physically accessible for every user. For example, sidewalks are designed with curb cuts so that people using wheelchairs can access the sidewalk. However, because the design is available in the environment for anyone to use, many others benefit: parents pushing strollers, travelers rolling suitcases, bikers, roller-bladers, and delivery personnel maneuvering dollies loaded with packages. UDL incorporated this same thinking but for the design of curricular goals, assessments, materials, methods, and physical classroom spaces.

Universal Design for Learning

Universal Design for Learning is a framework to proactively design learning environments that support the range of learners we know we will have in our classrooms (Meyer, Rose, & Gordon, 2014). The three UDL principles align with three broad learning networks in the brain, and the nine UDL guidelines and associated checkpoints provide an organized way to align best teaching practices and learning strategies. Educators already incorporate these practices and strategies, but the intentionality shifts with UDL.

UDL provides a common language for students and educators to use around learning that is asset-based. A student once remarked, "I have all of those brain networks," which differed from previous approaches that labeled and described deficits. The UDL checkpoints align with best-practice resources, tools, and strategies that educators can share with their learners, parents, and one another. It provides a common language around teaching and learning that is invaluable for collaboration, reflection, deepened understanding, and design. You can turn all of the UDL checkpoints into questions to reflect upon your design. However, note that you do not need to include every UDL checkpoint in a lesson—focus on ones that reduce barriers to achieve the intended goal.

UDL puts the burden of change on the design of the learning environment, so we analyze the environment and not the individual. There is a horizontal organization to the UDL guidelines that aligns to designing for access; skill building; and independent, internalized learning. UDL defines as its ultimate goal the development of "expert learners" who are purposeful and motivated, resourceful and knowledgeable, and strategic and goal-directed. This expert learner will look different and be defined uniquely across different disciplines and developmental ages.

There is also a vertical organization of the UDL guidelines that aligns to the learning brain (as described in Chapter 2). Options for engagement include learning goals, assessments, materials, and methods that recruit interest, help sustain effort and persistence through challenges, and self-regulate and self-reflect on the learning. Options for representation include goals, assessments, materials, and methods that help learners perceive, build language, and comprehend information. These strategies often align to content delivery methods, such as the use of whiteboards, lectures, PowerPoint presentations, videos, word walls, or concept maps. Options for action and expression support learners in providing options for how they can demonstrate what they know and may include goals, assessments, materials, and methods such as computers, manipulatives, calculators, graphic organizers, sentence starters, templates, model examples, and checklists.

A quick assessment of your lesson or learning experience using the UDL framework can reveal whether the current resources align with and support the learning goals, as well as whether they reduce barriers or scaffold learning. A quick way to use the UDL framework is to ask the following questions of a lesson or learning event:

- What is the goal of the lesson/learning experience?
- What options for engagement, representation, and action and expression are already present in the lesson and work well?
- What additional options for engagement, representation, and action and expression could be incorporated to reduce some

of the barriers that typically prevent learners from achieving the goal? For example, where do you have to reteach or where do your learners typically get stuck?

Start your design at those places. You may think of an individual and the barrier that will prevent this student from achieving the goal when using UDL to plan and design. However, make the design option available at the start of the lesson, available in the environment, and for all learners to use. You may have a student who has reading challenges, so you'd provide an audio option for a reading with this student in mind—but it should be one that any student could use in service of the goal. Like the curb cut in architecture, the design is in the environment from the beginning for all to access.

A Challenge for Educators

Integrating choices into lessons can be a time-consuming task. With a large course load, many students, and limited time, how can educators also do this? Start small! For example, you could add just one choice into one part of a lesson (affectionately called a "UDL + 1"). In subsequent lessons, you may choose additional options aligned to your goal and that reduce construct-irrelevant barriers for your learners. A college professor offers the following encouragement: "The design may take longer the first time, but it will get easier, and the next time you have that lesson, it will be better. In addition, if students are more engaged in active learning, you will likely save time because you won't have to reteach as much."

Reframe the nine UDL guidelines and associated checkpoints to be questions. Reflect on tools, resources, and strategies you already have (or open up your cabinets and see how you might reconfigure or integrate tools you already have to serve a learning goal). Think of designing a "learning buffet" of relevant options for learners to reduce barriers toward the goal. Remember that you do not need to incorporate all of the UDL guidelines in a single lesson; instead, you should focus on the ones that reduce barriers toward your intended goals. For more information and ideas about the UDL guidelines, please visit http://udlguidelines.cast.org, and for more information about CAST, the organization that founded the UDL Guidelines, visit www.cast.org.

- UDL is not "just good teaching." It allows us to be proactive, purposeful, and reflective in very concrete ways. It aligns our best practices within the learning brain networks and focuses first on access and engagement.

- UDL gives educators, students, and parents a common language for learning.

- UDL can be integrated by all educators in all roles. For example, administrators can design faculty meetings or parents' nights using UDL. Educators have redesigned campus tours, cafeteria management, and registration procedures using the UDL framework.

- UDL aligns with initiatives you may already have at your school. For example, once you have designed your "learning buffet" using the UDL guidelines to reduce barriers toward a goal, it is easier to differentiate or personalize instruction. UDL provides the "how," and standards or competencies can provide the "what" of the goal.

- UDL encourages educators to first make their design accessible, through options for perception, physical action, and interest. With those, deeper learning toward comprehension, executive function, and self-regulation is possible. From the outset, learning should be accessible for all.

BIBLIOGRAPHY

Aminoff, E. M., Kveraga, K., & Bar, M. (2013). The role of the parahippocampal cortex in cognition. *Trends in Cognitive Sciences, 17*(8), 379–390.

Arain, M., Haque, M., Johal, L., Mathur, P., Nel, W., Rais, A., et al. (2013). Maturation of the adolescent brain. *Neuropsychiatric Disease and Treatment, 9,* 449–461.

Armstrong, T. (2010). *Neurodiversity: Discovering the extraordinary gifts of autism, ADHD, dyslexia, and other brain differences.* Cambridge, MA: Da Capo Press.

Aronson, E., Wilson, T. D., & Akert, R. M. (2005). *Social psychology* (7th ed.). Upper Saddle River, NJ: Pearson.

Aronson, J., Fried, C. B., & Good, C. (2002). Reducing the effects of stereotype threat on African American college students by shaping theories of intelligence. *Journal of Experimental Social Psychology, 38*(2), 113–125.

Atkinson, R. K., Derry, S. J., Renkl, A., & Wortham, D. (2000). Learning from examples: Instructional principles from the worked examples research. *Review of Educational Research, 70*(2), 181–214.

Awh, E., & Jonides, J. (2001). Overlapping mechanisms of attention and spatial working memory. *Trends in Cognitive Sciences, 5*(3), 119–126.

Baddeley, A. (2000). The episodic buffer: A new component of working memory? *Trends in Cognitive Sciences, 4*(11), 417–423.

Baddeley, A. (2003). Working memory and language: An overview. *Journal of Communication Disorders, 36*(3), 189–208.

Baddeley, A., Gathercole, S., & Papagno, C. (1998). The phonological loop as a language learning device. *Psychological Review, 105*(1), 158–173.

Baldassano, C., Beck, D. M., & Fei-Fei, L. (2013). Differential connectivity within the Parahippocampal Place Area. *Neuroimage, 75,* 228–237.

Banich, M. T. (2004). *Cognitive neuroscience and neuropsychology.* Boston: Houghton Mifflin.

Barrett, L. F. (2017a). *How emotions are made.* New York: Houghton Mifflin.

Barrett, L. F. (2017b). The theory of constructed emotion: An active inference account of interoception and categorization. *Social Cognitive and Affective Neuroscience, 12*(1), 1–23.

Barrett, L. F., & Simmons, W. K. (2015). Interoceptive predictions in the brain. *Nature Reviews Neuroscience, 16*(7), 419–429.

Barrouillet, P., Bernardin, S., Portrat, S., Vergauwe, E., & Camos, V. (2007). Time and cognitive load in working memory. *Journal of Experimental Psychology: Learning, Memory, and Cognition, 33*(3), 570–585.

Battro, A. (2000). *Half a brain is enough: The story of Nico.* Cambridge, UK: Cambridge University Press.

Battro, A. M. (2010). The teaching brain. *Mind, Brain, and Education, 4*(1), 28–33.

Bear, M. F., Connors, B. W., & Paradiso, M. A. (2007). *Neuroscience: Exploring the brain* (3rd ed.). Baltimore: Lippincott Williams & Wilkins.

Bechara, A., Damasio, H., Tranel, D., & Damasio, A. R. (2005). The Iowa gambling task and the somatic marker hypothesis: Some questions and answers. *Trends in Cognitive Neuroscience, 9*(4) 159–162.

Benítez, P. F., Verdejo, J., León, P., Reimerink, A., & Guzmán, G. (2014). Neural substrates of specialized knowledge representation: An fMRI study. *Revue Française de Linguistique Appliquée, 19*(1), 15–32.

Bernardi, G., Ricciardi, E., Sani, L., Gaglianese, A., Papasogli, A., Ceccarelli, R., et al. (2013). How skill expertise shapes the brain functional architecture: An fMRI study of visuo-spatial and motor processing in professional racing-car and naïve drivers. *PLoS ONE, 8*(10): e77764.

Beyerstein, B. L. (1999). Whence cometh the myth that we only use ten percent of our brains? In S. Della Sala (Ed.), *Mind myths: Exploring everyday mysteries of the mind and brain* (pp. 1–24). Chichester, UK: Wiley.

Bidell, T. R., & Fischer, K. W. (1992). Beyond the stage debate: Action, structure, and variability in Piagetian theory and research. In R. J. Sternberg & C. A. Berg (Eds.), *Intellectual development* (pp. 100–140). New York: Cambridge University Press.

Black, A. E., & Deci, E. L. (2000). The effects of instructors' autonomy support and students' autonomous motivation on learning organic chemistry: A self-determination theory perspective. *Science Education, 84*(6), 740–756.

Borod, J. C. (Ed.). (2000). *The neuropsychology of emotion.* New York: Oxford University Press.

Britton, B. K., Holdredge, T. S., Curry, C., & Westbrook, R. D. (1979). Use of cognitive capacity in reading identical texts with different amounts of discourse level meaning. *Journal of Experimental Psychology: Human Learning and Memory, 5*(3), 262–270.

Bruer, J. T. (1997). Education and the brain: A bridge too far. *Educational Researcher, 26*(8), 4–16. Retrieved from www.jsmf.org/about/j/education_and_brain.pdf

Cerebralpalsy.org. (n.d.). Artists with cerebral palsy: Paul Smith. Retrieved from www.cerebralpalsy.org/inspiration/artists/paul-smith

Chabris, C., & Simons, D. (2010). *The invisible gorilla: And other ways our intuitions deceive us.* New York: Crown.

Christoff, K., Gordon, A. M., Smallwood, J., Smith, R., & Schooler, J. W. (2009). Experience sampling during fMRI reveals default network and executive system contributions to mind wandering. *Proceedings of the National Academy of Sciences of the United States of America, 106*(21), 8719–8724.

Cohen, G. L., Garcia, J., Purdie-Vaughns, V., Apfel, N., & Brzustoski, P. (2009). Recursive processes in self-affirmation: Intervening to close the minority achievement gap. *Science, 324*(5925), 400–403.

Corbetta, M., & Shulman, G. L. (2002). Control of goal-directed and stimulus-driven attention in the brain. *Nature Reviews Neuroscience, 3*(3), 201–215.

Craig, A. D. (2008). Interoception and emotion: A neuroanatomical perspective. In M. Lewis, J. M. Haviland-Jones, & L. F. Barrett (Eds.), *Handbook of emotions* (pp. 272–288). New York: Guilford Press.

Csikszentmihalyi, M. (1997). *Finding flow: The psychology of engagement with everyday life.* New York: Basic Books.

Curcio, C. A., & Allen, K. A. (1990). Topography of ganglion cells in human retina. *Journal of Comparative Neurology, 300*(1), 5–25.

Daley, S. G., Willett, J. B., & Fischer, K. W. (2014). Emotional responses during reading: Physiological responses predict real-time reading comprehension. *Journal of Educational Psychology, 106*(1), 132–143.

Dalgleish, T., and Power, M. (Eds.). (1999). *Handbook of cognition and emotion.* New York: Wiley.

Damasio, A. (1994). *Descartes' error: Emotion, reason, and the human brain*. New York: Putnam.

Damasio, A. R., Damasio, H., & Van Hoesen, G. W. (1982). Prosopagnosia: Anatomic basis and behavioral mechanisms. *Neurology, 32*(4), 331–341.

Deci, E. L., & Ryan, R. M. (2008). Self-determination theory: A macrotheory of human motivation, development, and health. *Canadian psychology/Psychologie canadienne, 49*(3), 182.

Deci, E. L., & Ryan, R. M. (2012). Self-determination theory. In P. A. M. Van Lange, A. W. Kruglanski, & E. T. Higgins (Eds.), *Handbook of theories of social psychology* (Vol. 1, pp. 416–437). Thousand Oaks, CA: Sage.

Dekker, S., Lee, N. C., Howard-Jones, P., & Jolles, J. (2012). Neuromyths in education: Prevalence and predictors of misconceptions among teachers. *Frontiers in Psychology, 3*, 429.

Diamond, M. C., Scheibel, A. B., Murphy, G. M., & Harvey, T. (1985). On the brain of a scientist: Albert Einstein. *Experimental Neurology, 88*(1), 198–204.

Doidge, N. (2007). *The brain that changes itself: Stories of personal triumph from the frontiers of brain science*. New York: Penguin.

Drew, T., Võ, M. L.-H., & Wolfe, J. M. (2013). The invisible gorilla strikes again: Sustained inattentional blindness in expert observers. *Psychological Science, 24*(9), 1848–1853.

Dufour, R. (2012). When districts function as professional learning communities. *The Education Digest, 77*(9), 28.

Dündar, S., & Gündüz, N. (2016). Misconceptions regarding the brain: The neuromyths of preservice teachers. *Mind, Brain, and Education, 10*(4), 212–232.

Dweck, C. S. (2007, October). The perils and promises of praise. *Educational Leadership, 65*(2), 34–39.

Epstein, R., Harris, A., Stanley, D., & Kanwisher, N. (1999). The parahippocampal place area: Recognition, navigation, or encoding? *Neuron, 23*(1), 115–125.

Facoetti, A., Paganoni, P., & Lorusso, M. L. (2000). The spatial distribution of visual attention in developmental dyslexia. *Experimental Brain Research, 132*(4), 531–538.

Falk, D. (2009). New information about Albert Einstein's brain. *Frontiers in Evolutionary Neuroscience, 1*(3).

Fallon, J. (2013). *The psychopath inside: A neuroscientist's personal journey into the dark side of the brain.* New York: Penguin.

Feldman, L. A. (1995). Valence focus and arousal focus: Individual differences in the structure of affective experience. *Journal of Personality and Social Psychology, 69*(1), 153–166.

Fraga, M. F., Ballestar, E., Paz, M. F., Ropero, S., Setien, F., Ballestar, M. L., et al. (2005). Epigenetic differences arise during the lifetime of monozygotic twins. *Proceedings of the National Academy of Sciences of the United States of America, 102*(30), 10604–10609.

Gagne, M., & Deci, E. L. (2005). Self-determination theory and work motivation. *Journal of Organizational Behavior, 26*(4), 331–362.

Giuliano, R. J., Pfordresher, P. Q., Stanley, E. M., Narayana, S., & Wicha, N. Y. (2011). Native experience with a tone language enhances pitch discrimination and the timing of neural responses to pitch change. *Frontiers in Psychology, 2*, 146.

Gould, E., Beylin, A., Tanapat, P., Reeves, A., & Shors, T. J. (1999). Learning enhances adult neurogenesis in the hippocampal formation. *Nature Neuroscience, 2*(3), 260–265.

Gray, L., & Taie, S., (2015). *Public school teacher attrition and mobility in the first five years.* Washington, DC: National Center for Education Statistics. Retrieved from http://nces.ed.gov/pubs2015/2015337.pdf

Graziano, C. (2005, February 9). Public education faces a crisis in teacher retention. *Edutopia*. Retrieved from www.edutopia.org/schools-out

Hagerty, B. B. (2010, June 29). A neuroscientist uncovers a dark secret. NPR.org/templates/story/story.php?storyId=127888976

Hall, T. E., Meyer, A., & Rose, D. H. (Eds.). (2012). *Universal design for learning in the classroom: Practical application.* Chicago: Guilford.

Hara, Y. (2015). Brain plasticity and rehabilitation in stroke patients. *Journal of Nippon Medical School, 82*(1), 4–13.

Herculano-Houzel, S. (2009). The human brain in numbers: A linearly scaled-up primate brain. *Frontiers in Human Neuroscience, 3,* 31.

Herholz, S. C., & Zatorre, R. J. (2012). Musical training as a framework for brain plasticity: Behavior, function, and structure. *Neuron, 76*(3), 486–502.

Hillman, C. H., Pontifex, M. B., Raine, L. B., Castelli, D. M., Hall, E. E., & Kramer, A. F. (2009). The effect of acute treadmill walking on cognitive control and academic achievement in preadolescent children. *Neuroscience, 159*(3), 1044–1054.

Immordino-Yang, M. H. (2008). The smoke around mirror neurons: Goals as sociocultural and emotional organizers of perception and action in learning. *Mind, Brain, and Education, 2*(2), 67–73.

Immordino-Yang, M. H. (2011). Implications of affective and social neuroscience for educational theory. *Educational Philosophy and Theory, 43*(1), 98–103.

Immordino-Yang, M. H. (2015). *Emotions, learning, and the brain: Exploring the educational implications of affective neuroscience.* Norton Series on the Social Neuroscience of Education. New York: Norton.

Immordino-Yang, M. H., Christodoulou, J. A., & Singh, V. (2012). Rest is not idleness: Implications of the brain's default mode for human development and education. *Perspectives on Psychological Science, 7*(4), 352–364.

Immordino-Yang, M. H., & Damasio, A. (2007). We feel therefore we learn: The relevance of affective and social neuroscience to education. *Mind, Brain, and Education, 1*(1) 3–10.

Immordino-Yang, M. H., & Faeth, M. (2010). The role of emotion and skilled intuition in learning. *Mind, brain, and education: Neuroscience implications for the classroom, 69,* 83.

Jamieson, J. P., Mendes, W. B., & Nock, M. K. (2013). Improving acute stress responses: The power of reappraisal. *Current Directions in Psychological Science, 22*(1), 51–56.

Jang, H., Reeve, J., & Deci, E. L. (2010). Engaging students in learning activities: It is not autonomy support or structure but autonomy support and structure. *Journal of Educational Psychology, 102*(3), 588–600.

Jarrold, C., & Towse, J. N. (2006). Individual differences in working memory. *Neuroscience, 139*(1), 39–50.

Jung-Beeman, M., Collier, A., & Kounios, J. (2008). How insight happens: Learning from the brain. *NeuroLeadership Journal 1*(1), 20–25.

Kang, Y. H., Petzschner, F. H., Wolpert, D. M., & Shadlen, M. N. (2017). Piercing of consciousness as a threshold-crossing operation. *Current Biology, 27*(15), 2285–2295.

Kato, N., & McEwen, B. (2003). Neuromechanisms of emotions and memory. *Neuroendocrinology, 11*(03), 54–58.

Kauffman, T., Théoret, H., & Pascual-Leone, A. (2002). Braille character discrimination in blindfolded human subjects. *Neuroreport, 13*(5), 571–574.

Klimesch, W. (2012). Alpha-band oscillations, attention, and controlled access to stored information. *Trends in Cognitive Sciences, 16*(12), 606–617.

Long, P., & Corfas, G. (2014). To learn is to myelinate. *Science, 346*(6207), 298–299.

Luria, A. R. (1968). *The mind of a mnemonist: A little book about a vast memory.* Cambridge, MA: Harvard University Press.

Lynch, M. A. (2004). Long-term potentiation and memory. *Physiological Reviews, 84*(1), 87–136.

Maguire, E. A., Gadian, D. G., Johnsrude, I. S., Good, C. D., Ashburner, J., Frackowiak, R. S., & Frith, C. D. (2000). Navigation-related structural change in the hippocampi of taxi drivers. *Proceedings of the National Academy of Sciences of the United States of America, 97*(8), 4398–4403.

Maguire, E. A., Woollett, K., & Spiers, H. J. (2006). London taxi drivers and bus drivers: A structural MRI and neuropsychological analysis. *Hippocampus, 16*(12), 1091–1101.

Mareschal, D., Johnson, M. H., Sirois, S., Spratling, M. W., Thomas, M. S., & Westermann, G. (2007). *Neuroconstructivism: How the brain constructs cognition* (Vol. 1). New York: Oxford University Press.

Marx, D. M., Sei, J. K., & Friedman, R. A. (2009). The "Obama effect": How a salient role model reduces race-based performance differences. *Journal of Experimental Social Psychology, 45*(4), 953–956.

Mauguière, F., & Corkin, S. (2015). H.M. never again! An analysis of H.M.'s epilepsy and treatment. *Revue neurologique, 171*(3), 273–281.

McGaugh, J. L. (2015). Consolidating memories. *Annual Review of Psychology, 66,* 1–24.

McGaugh, J. L., Cahill, L., & Roozendaal, B. (1996). Involvement of the amygdala in memory storage: Interaction with other brain systems. *Proceedings of the National Academy of Sciences of the United States of America, 93*(24), 13508–13514.

Mehta, D., Klengel, T., Conneely, K. N., Smith, A. K., Altmann, A., Pace, T. W., et al. (2013). Childhood maltreatment is associated with distinct genomic and epigenetic profiles in posttraumatic stress disorder. *Proceedings of the National Academy of Sciences of the United States of America, 110*(20), 8302–8307.

Meltzoff, A. N., & Moore, M. K. (1997). Explaining facial imitation: A theoretical model. *Early Development & Parenting, 6*(3–4), 179–192.

Mendoza, J., & Foundas, A. (2007). *Clinical neuroanatomy: A neurobehavioral approach.* New York: Springer Science & Business Media.

Meo, G. (2008). Curriculum planning for all learners: Applying Universal Design for Learning (UDL) to a high school reading comprehension program. *Preventing School Failure 52*(2), 21–30.

Meyer, A., Rose, D. H., & Gordon, D. (2014). *Universal design for learning: Theory and practice.* Wakefield, MA: CAST Professional Publishing.

Nakamura, J., & Csikszentmihalyi, M. (2014). The concept of flow. In M. Csikszentmihalyi, *Flow and the foundations of positive psychology* (pp. 239–263). Chicago: Springer Netherlands.

Nathanson, L., Rivers, S. E., Flynn, L. M., & Brackett, M. A. (2016). Creating emotionally intelligent schools with RULER. *Emotion Review, 8*(4), 305–310.

National Research Council and Institute of Medicine (2004). *Engaging schools: Fostering high school students' motivation to learn.* Executive Summary. Washington, DC: National Academies Press. Retrieved from www.nap.edu/openbook.php?record_id=10421&page=4

Novak, K. (2014). *UDL now! A teacher's Monday morning guide to implementing the Common Core Standards using Universal Design for Learning.* Wakefield, MA: CAST Professional Publishing.

O'Driscoll, K., & Leach, J. P. (1998). "No longer Gage": An iron bar through the head: Early observations of personality change after injury to the prefrontal cortex. *BMJ, 317*(7174), 1673–1674.

Ornstein, R. (1992). *Evolution of consciousness: The origins of the way we think*. New York: Simon and Schuster.

Paas, F., Renkl, A., & Sweller, J. (2010). Cognitive load theory and instructional design: Recent developments. *Educational psychologist, 38*(1), 1–4.

Paquette, V., Lévesque, J., Mensour, B., Leroux, J. M., Beaudoin, G., Bourgouin, P., & Beauregard, M. (2003). "Change the mind and you change the brain": Effects of cognitive-behavioral therapy on the neural correlates of spider phobia. *Neuroimage, 18*(2), 401–409.

Park, S., & Chun, M. M. (2009). Different roles of the parahippocampal place area (PPA) and retrosplenial cortex (RSC) in panoramic scene perception. *NeuroImage, 47*(4), 1747–1756.

Peifer, C., Schulz, A., Schachinger, H., Baumann, N., Antoni, C. H. (2014). The relation of flow-experience and psychological arousal under stress—Can u shape it? *Journal of Experimental Social Psychology, 53*, 62–69. Retrieved from www.sciencedirect.com/science/article/pii/S0022103114000109

Pring, L., Hermelin, B., Buhler, M., & Walker, I. (1997). Native savant talent and acquired skill. *Autism, 1*(2), 199–214.

Quiroga, R. Q. (2014). *The man who could not forget: A BIT of Borges and memory*. Cambridge, MA: MIT Press.

Quiroga, R. Q., Reddy, L., Kreiman, G., Koch, C., & Fried, I. (2005). Invariant visual representation by single neurons in the human brain. *Nature, 435*(7045), 1102–1107.

Ramachandran, V. S. (2003). *The emerging mind: The Reith Lectures*. London: Profile Books.

Ramachandran, V. S., Blakeslee, S., & Shah, N. (1998). *Phantoms in the brain: Probing the mysteries of the human mind*. New York: Morrow.

Reeves, B., & Nass, C. (1996). *The media equation: How people treat computers, television, and new media like real people and places*. New York: Cambridge University Press.

Repovš, G., & Baddeley, A. (2006). The multi-component model of working memory: Explorations in experimental cognitive psychology. *Neuroscience, 139*(1), 5–21.

Riener, C. R., Stefanucci, J. K., Proffitt, D. R., & Clore, G. L. (2011). An effect of mood on the perception of geographical slant. *Cognition and Emotion, 25*(1), 174–182.

Riener, C., & Willingham, D. (2010). The myth of learning styles. *Change: The Magazine of Higher Learning, 42*(5), 32–35.

Rodrigues, S. M., LeDoux, J. E., & Sapolsky, R. M. (2009). The influence of stress hormones on fear circuitry. *Annual Review of Neuroscience, 32,* 289–313.

Ryan, R. M., & Deci, E. L. (2000). Self-determination theory and the facilitation of intrinsic motivation, social development, and well-being. *American Psychologist, 55*(1), 68–78. Retrieved from http://selfdeterminationtheory.org/SDT/documents/2000_Ryan Deci_SDT.pdf

Sapolsky, R. M. (2004). *Why zebras don't get ulcers* (3rd ed.). New York: Times Books.

Scherer, K. R., Schorr, A., & Johnstone, T. (Eds.). (2001). *Appraisal processes in emotion: Theory, methods, research.* New York: Oxford University Press.

Schlegel, A. A., Rudelson, J. J., & Tse, P. U. (2012). White matter structure changes as adults learn a second language. *Journal of Cognitive Neuroscience, 24*(8), 1664–1670.

Schmidt, J. A., Shumow, L., & Kackar-Cam, H. Z. (2017). Does mindset intervention predict students' daily experience in classrooms? A comparison of seventh and ninth graders' trajectories. *Journal of Youth and Adolescence, 46*(3), 582–602.

Schneps, M. H., Rose, T., & Fischer, K. W. (2007). Visual learning and the brain: Implications for dyslexia. *Mind, Brain, and Education, 1*(3), 128–139.

Schwartz, B. (2004). *The paradox of choice: Why more is less.* New York: HarperCollins.

Seung, S. (2012). *Connectome: How the brain's wiring makes us who we are.* New York: Houghton Mifflin Harcourt.

Shapiro, A., Lu, Z. L., Huang, C. B., Knight, E., & Ennis, R. (2010). Transitions between central and peripheral vision create spatial/temporal distortions: A hypothesis concerning the perceived break of the curveball. *PLoS One, 5*(10), e13296.

Shernoff, D. J., Csikszentmihalyi, M., Schneider, B., & Shernoff, E. S. (2014). Student engagement in high school classrooms from the perspective of flow theory. In *Applications of Flow in Human Development and Education* (pp. 475–494). Chicago: Springer Netherlands.

Shumow, L., & Schmidt, J. A. (2014). *Enhancing adolescents' motivation for science: Research-based strategies for teaching male and female students.* Thousand Oaks, CA: Corwin.

Sisson, K. L. (2009). Learning styles challenged: Data don't support popular learning theory. Retrieved January 31, 2015, from www.psychologicalscience.org/media/releases/2009/learning stylespspi.cfm

Skoe, E., & Chandrasekaran, B. (2014). The layering of auditory experiences in driving experience-dependent subcortical plasticity. *Hearing Research, 311,* 36–48.

Stanley, M. L., Moussa, M. N., Paolini, B. M., Lyday, R. G., Burdette, J. H., & Laurienti, P. J. (2013). Defining nodes in complex brain networks. *Frontiers in Computational Neuroscience, 7,* 169.

Steele, C. M. (1997). A threat in the air: How stereotypes shape intellectual identity and performance. *American Psychologist, 52*(6), 613–629.

Stefanucci, J. K., Gagnon K. T., & Lessard, D. (2011). Follow your heart: Emotion adaptively influences perception. *Social and Personality Psychology Compass, 5*(6): 296–308.

Subramaniam, K., Kounios, J., Parrish, T. B., & Jung-Beeman, M. (2009). A brain mechanism for facilitation of insight by positive affect. *Journal of Cognitive Neuroscience, 21*(3), 415–432.

Supekar, K., Uddin, L. Q., Khouzam, A., Phillips, J., Gaillard, W. D., Kenworthy, L. E., et al. (2013). Brain hyperconnectivity in children with autism and its links to social deficits. *Cell Reports, 5*(3), 738–747.

Sweller, J. (1994). Cognitive load theory, learning difficulty, and instructional design. *Learning and Instruction, 4*(4), 295–312.

Tammet, D. (2006). *Born on a blue day: Inside the extraordinary mind of an autistic savant.* New York: Free Press.

Thiel, C. M., Studte, S., Hildebrandt, H., Huster, R., & Weerda, R. (2014). When a loved one feels unfamiliar: A case study on the neural basis of Capgras delusion. *Cortex, 52,* 75–85.

Tominey, S. L., O'Bryon, E. C., Rivers, S. E., & Shapses, S. (2017). Teaching emotional intelligence in early childhood. *Young Children, 72*(1).

Tomporowski, P. D. (2003). Effects of acute bouts of exercise on cognition. *Acta Psychologica, 112*(3), 297–324.

Treffert, D. A. (2009). The savant syndrome: An extraordinary condition. A synopsis: Past, present, future. *Philosophical Transactions of the Royal Society of London B: Biological Sciences, 364*(1522), 1351–1357.

Twomey, S. (2010, January). Phineas Gage: Neuroscience's most famous patient. *Smithsonian.*

Two-time world memory champion Wang Feng explains his phenomenal memory. (2013, February 5). YouTube. Retrieved from www.youtube.com/watch?v=Az5Mvs5DTzc

UC San Diego School of Medicine. (n.d.). What is fMRI? Retrieved from http://fmri.ucsd.edu/Research/whatisfmri.html

Uddin, L. Q., Supekar, K., & Menon, V. (2013). Reconceptualizing functional brain connectivity in autism from a developmental perspective. *Frontiers in Human Neuroscience, 7,* 458.

Van Geert, P., & Steenbeek, H. (2008). Brains and the dynamics of "wants" and "cans" in learning. *Mind, Brain, and Education, 2*(2), 62–66.

Van Gorp, T., & Adams, E. (2012). *Design for emotion.* Waltham, MA: Elsevier.

Vygotsky, L. (1978). Interaction between learning and development. In M. Gauvain & M. Cole (Eds.), *Readings on the development of children* (pp. 34–40). New York: Scientific American Books.

Waterland, R. A., & Jirtle, R. L. (2003). Transposable elements: Targets for early nutritional effects on epigenetic gene regulation. *Molecular and Cellular Biology, 23*(15), 5293–5300.

Willingham, D. T., Hughes, E. M., & Dobolyi, D. G. (2015). The scientific status of learning styles theories. *Teaching of Psychology, 42*(3), 266–271.

Willis, J. (2006). *Research-based strategies to ignite student learning: Insights from a neurologist and classroom teacher.* Alexandria, VA: ASCD.

Willis, J. (2007). Brain-based teaching strategies for improving students' memory, learning, and test-taking success. *Childhood Education, 83*(5), 310–315.

Wright, H. H., & Shisler, R. J. (2005). Working memory in aphasia: Theory, measures, and clinical implications. *American Journal of Speech-Language Pathology, 14*(2), 107–118.

Yang, X. F., Bossmann, J., Schiffhauer, B., Jordan, M., & Immordino-Yang, M. H. (2012). Intrinsic default mode network connectivity predicts spontaneous verbal descriptions of autobiographical memories during social processing. *Frontiers in Psychology, 3,* 592.

Yeager, D. S., Purdie-Vaughns, V., Garcia, J., Apfel, N., Brzustoski, P., Master, A., et al. (2014). Breaking the cycle of mistrust: Wise interventions to provide critical feedback across the racial divide. *Journal of Experimental Psychology: General, 143*(2), 804–824.

Zadra, J. R., & Clore, G. L. (2011). Emotion and perception: The role of affective information. *Wiley Interdisciplinary Reviews: Cognitive Science, 2*(6), 676–685.

Zatorre, R. J., Fields, R. D., & Johansen-Berg, H. (2012). Plasticity in gray and white: Neuroimaging changes in brain structure during learning. *Nature Neuroscience, 15*(4), 528–536.

INDEX

The letter *f* following a page number denotes a figure.

ABOUT THE AUTHOR

Allison Posey is a curriculum and design specialist at CAST, the Center for Applied Special Technology. There, she engages in curricular design, leads professional development trainings for the Universal Design for Learning framework, and supports online course instruction, including the UDL Affect and Engagement course. She works with educators across the United States and internationally to integrate and apply current understandings from brain research about learning into instructional practices so that all learners can engage in rigorous learning opportunities. She coordinates the CAST free webinar series and presents on the central role of emotions in learning.

Before her work at CAST, Allison was a life science teacher in middle school, high school, and community college settings, teaching genetics, anatomy, physiology, biology, neuroscience, and psychology. She received a degree in Mind, Brain, and Education from the Harvard Graduate School of Education, where she also worked as a teaching fellow for courses such as "Educational Neuroscience" and "Framing

Scientific Research for Public Understanding." She holds a certificate in fine arts from the Maryland Institute of Art. Her favorite pastimes are hiking and biking, painting, watching sunsets, and learning about the brain with her friends and family.

Allison can be found on Twitter @AllisonAPosey.

Related ASCD Resources

At the time of publication, the following resources were available (ASCD stock numbers in parentheses).

Print Products

Attack of the Teenage Brain! Understanding and Supporting the Weird and Wonderful Adolescent Learner by John Medina (#118024)

The Brain-Compatible Classroom: Using What We Know About Learning to Improve Teaching by Laura Erlauer (#101269)

Brain Matters: Translating Research into Classroom Practice, 2nd Edition by Patricia Wolfe (#109073)

Building Learning Communities with Character: How to Integrate Academic, Social, and Emotional Learning by Bernard Novick, Jeffrey S. Kress, and Maurice J. Elias (#101240)

Differentiation and the Brain: How Neuroscience Supports the Learner-Friendly Classroom, 2nd Edition by David A. Sousa and Carol Ann Tomlinson (#318125)

Handling Student Frustrations: How Do I Help Students Manage Emotions in the Classroom? by Renate Caine and Carol McClintic (#SF114068)

The Motivated Brain: Improving Student Attention, Engagement, and Perseverance by Gayle Gregory and Martha Kaufeldt (#115041)

The Power of the Adolescent Brain: Strategies for Teaching Middle and High School Students by Thomas Armstrong (#116017)

Self-Regulated Learning for Academic Success: How Do I Help Students Manage Their Thoughts, Behaviors, and Emotions? by Carrie Germeroth and Crystal Day-Hess (#SF114041)

Teaching Students to Drive Their Brains: Metacognitive Strategies, Activities, and Lesson Ideas by Donna Wilson and Marcus Conyers (#117002)

Teaching with the Brain in Mind, 2nd Edition by Eric Jensen (#104013)

ASCD myTeachSource®

Download resources from a professional learning platform with hundreds of research-based best practices and tools for your classroom at http://myteachsource.ascd.org/

For more information, send an e-mail to member@ascd.org; call 1-800-933-2723 or 703-578-9600; send a fax to 703-575-5400; or write to Information Services, ASCD, 1703 N. Beauregard St., Alexandria, VA 22311-1714 USA.

WHOLE CHILD
TENETS

The ASCD Whole Child approach is an effort to transition from a focus on narrowly defined academic achievement to one that promotes the long-term development and success of all children. Through this approach, ASCD supports educators, families, community members, and policymakers as they move from a vision about educating the whole child to sustainable, collaborative actions.

Engage the Brain relates to the **supported**, **healthy**, and **engaged** tenets.
*For more about the ASCD Whole Child approach, visit **www.ascd.org/wholechild**.*

1 **HEALTHY**
Each student enters school healthy and learns about and practices a healthy lifestyle.

2 **SAFE**
Each student learns in an environment that is physically and emotionally safe for students and adults.

3 **ENGAGED**
Each student is actively engaged in learning and is connected to the school and broader community.

4 **SUPPORTED**
Each student has access to personalized learning and is supported by qualified, caring adults.

5 **CHALLENGED**
Each student is challenged academically and prepared for success in college or further study and for employment and participation in a global environment.